Race, Politics, and Economic Development

THE HAYMARKET SERIES

Editors: Mike Davis and Michael Sprinker

The Haymarket Series offers original studies in politics, history and culture, with a focus on North America. Representing views across the American left on a wide range of subjects, the series will be of interest to socialists both in the USA and throughout the world. A century after the first May Day, the American left remains in the shadow of those martyrs whom the Haymarket Series honours and commemorates. These studies testify to the living legacy of political activism and commitment for which they gave their lives.

Race, Politics, and Economic Development

Community Perspectives

Edited by
JAMES JENNINGS

VERSO

London · New York

First published by Verso 1992
© Verso 1992
All rights reserved

Verso
UK: 6 Meard Street, London W1V 3HR
USA: 29 West 35th Street, New York, NY 10001-2291

Verso is the imprint of New Left Books

ISBN 0-86091-388-0
ISBN 0-86091-589-1 (pbk)

British Library Cataloguing in Publication Data
A catalogue record for this book is available from the British Library

Library of Congress Cataloging-in-Publication Data
A catalogue record for this book is available from the Library of Congress

Typeset by York House Typographic Ltd, London
Printed in Great Britain by Biddles Ltd, Guildford and Kings Lynn

Dedicated to
Lenora, Taha, Taleah-Esperanza,
Miriam, and Jadd

Contents

Acknowledgments

I would first like to thank all the contributors for their patience and perseverance in the final publication of this book. Nancy Murray, Ann Withorn, Bette Woody, William E. Nelson and Eugene Rivers read early drafts of various chapters and made many helpful suggestions.

Mike Davis and Michael Sprinker, editors at Verso, and Manning Marable, must also be acknowledged for their support and understanding of the importance of providing forums for Black scholars and activists who may not fit the "liberal" or "conservative" mode in the United States. Several individuals assisted me with editorial and logistical responsibilities. April Taylor, Christine Gomes and Benita Rheddick completed some of these tasks. Ilene Carver was very helpful in the final editing of this book. My thanks to all of these individuals.

Preface

William E. Nelson, Jr.

Since the turbulent decade of the 1960s a broad range of governmental programs have been constructed and implemented designed to address critical social and economic problems in the Black community. Despite the expenditure over the past two decades of massive amounts of public funds on urban development programs, the physical environment and the social and economic status of central city Black communities have continued to deteriorate. One theme of the powerful essays contained in this book is that recent public policies have failed to change appreciably the living conditions for millions of Black citizens because these policies are based on liberal and conservative analyses of American society that badly misconstrue the realities of Black community life.

This volume fills a crucial void in the social science framework underpinning the development of urban policy. The editor, Professor James Jennings of the University of Massachusetts and the William Monroe Trotter Institute, has assembled a group of talented Black scholars and political activists to provide unique perspectives in the debate about the content and direction of American urban policy. Rejecting the neo-colonial assumptions of both liberals and conservatives, these progressive Black voices provide penetrating insights into the systemic qualities of the American social and political order that have operated in the past as deterrents to the effective social, economic and political emergence of Black communities nationwide. The essays included here are pathbreaking; they move the discussion of the urban agenda well beyond the non-productive and distorted avenue of "blaming the victim," and suggest a multitude of new policy initiatives involving the participation of grassroots Black leaders in the process of policy development and implementation.

This is a book about political theory *and* political action. The authors of the articles in this volume clearly understand the pivotal need for contemporary Black scholars to become actively and permanently involved in the debate over public policy. Further, they recognize that the imperative of activist scholarship must be complemented by broadscale collective mobilization of the political, economic, social and cultural resources of the Black community. These are extremely important lessons. They tell us, for example, that ascension to high public offices by Black politicians in the cities cannot, as a singular strategy, address the multitudinous problems of the Black community. They also speak brilliantly to the inescapable fact that the dilemma of the continuing existence of a Black underclass in American cities will not be effectively tackled in the absence of a new vision of social reality, a radical rearrangement of power relations in the political arena, and the effective application of potential Black political strength to the process of governance at all levels of the American federal system. These insights will serve well future generations of community activists.

Introduction

James Jennings

Recent public policy related to Black economic and social development
has been conceptually and ideologically limited by two major schools
of thought, generally categorized as "liberal" and "neo-conservative."
Since the emergence of a literature by Black neo-conservatives and the
new reassertiveness of liberals as reflected in the publication of William
J. Wilson's *The Truly Disadvantaged: The Inner City, the Underclass,
and Public Policy* (1987) policy discussions and proposals to address
worsening social and economic conditions in Black urban communities
have generally excluded perspectives and ideas emerging from, and
reflecting, grassroots activist experiences. However, many community-
based ideas and social experiences cannot be conceptually fitted into
either the liberal or the neo-conservative schools of thought.

Writers reflecting both schools of thought have generally looked
down on or dismissed the ideas and insights of grassroots activists.
Thus Wilson laments how Black militants supposedly prevented Daniel
P. Moynihan from expressing fully his ideas about changes in Black
family structure.[1] As is typical of many Black neo-conservative writers,
Shelby Steele, in a more virulent way but lacking any analysis, also
disparages Black grassroots activists and intellectuals in his recent
prizewinning book, *The Content Of Our Character*.[2] There is now a
convergence of terminology and solutions regarding the problem of
Black social and economic development among liberals and conservatives, as is pointed out by Adolph Reed.[3] The neo-conservative school
is most typically represented in the works of Edward C. Banfield,
Thomas Sowell, Charles Murray and recently Shelby Steele.[4] The
liberal prognosis for Black community economic and social development is represented in the early works of Oscar Lewis, and later Ken
Auletta and William J. Wilson.[5]

There are, in fact, two other schools of thought regarding social and
economic development in urban America. One might be called "popu-

list" and the other "neo-Marxist." While the populist and Marxist-orientated framework proposed in works by Kenneth M. Dolbeare, William R. Tabb, Larry Sawers and others gained much attention during the 1970s and 1980s in the United States, its adherents have generally failed to provide practical policies related to the political and economic development of Black urban communities.[6] Many of these writers, while rejecting liberal and conservative urban and economic development paradigms, have nevertheless also overlooked the germane experiences of Blacks and Latinos involved in grassroots organizations.

One glaring example of this is an essay by Michael Peter Smith titled "The Uses of Linked-Development Policies in the U.S."[7] This is a case study of the adoption of a linkage program in Boston, Massachusetts, whereby downtown business developers assist in paying for the social costs of building in the downtown section of the city, by making a financial contribution to affordable housing and job training. This policy was adopted primarily as a result of mobilization in the Black community under the leadership of Black activist Mel King and others, including the first Black president of Boston's city council, Bruce Bolling. Ray Flynn, the populist who in 1983 replaced the pro-development Kevin White as mayor, endorsed and supported linkage – but only after the Black and progressive mayoral rival candidate Mel King organized the political momentum for this policy innovation. However, neither Mel King nor the impact that Black activism had on the adoption of linkage is ever mentioned in Smith's article. The author writes, furthermore, "Following White's decision not to seek reelection, all but one of the candidates for mayor ran on a pro-neighborhood campaign and supported linkage."[8] Here, Smith is referring to Flynn; but the fact of the matter is that the strongest pro-neighborhood candidate was Mel King. Campaign phrases utilized by King, as a matter of fact, were eventually adopted and used by Flynn.

Despite the predominance of liberal and neo-conservative ideas in mainstream scholarly arenas, there is still another general approach that has been offered by Black activists across the United States. Many of them, some writing about this topic more than a quarter of a century ago, have rejected liberal and neo-conservative assumptions and paradigms as responses to problems associated with Black economic and community development. Instead they have offered a range of policies and approaches to Black community development much broader than is suggested by the conventional public policy and ideological division between conservative and liberal policy advocates. A number of Black scholars and activists have both offered theoretical development models and also attempted to institutionalize social and economic strategies that reflect values, politics and even ideological characteristics different from those of the two dominant schools of thought.

Current liberal and neo-conservative public policy debates and forums do not present the range of institutional and political approaches that have been proposed by Black scholars and activists regarding social and economic development in the Black community. Some of the ideas and concerns of Black activists in the United States have also been overlooked by the mainstream media, and generally not treated seriously. But there is a body of literature and political thought that offers Black activist perspectives and ideas of community and economic development. This literature shows that ideas emerging from this source are approached differently than they are by liberal and conservative urbanists.

One example of this is how the continuing popularity and even reverence for the idea of "self-help" in the Black community has been misused. This idea, or value, has a long historical tradition among Blacks. One study reported, for example, that "the 'self-help' tradition is so embedded in the black heritage as to be virtually synonymous with it."[9] It can and has indeed served as an important political rallying call – as Black neo-conservatives have discovered. While neo-conservatives may contend that Black self-help economic and social initiatives are an appropriate response to deteriorating living conditions, the liberals simplistically argue that self-help is not adequate, and therefore opt for a benevolent, Keynesian-orientated government that responds to the needs of urban Blacks in emphasizing education and training, that is, human capital. Many liberals and neo-conservatives, however, fail to acknowledge or recognize the importance of the Black community's level of political power as a major determinant in getting government to become more responsive to their needs.

Absent from mainstream academic and policy debates between liberals and neo-conservatives is the perspective that posits the following: (a) self-help is critically important for Black economic and social development, but (b) Blacks have a fundamental right to expect their government to respond to their needs, and (c) the political mobilization and empowerment of Blacks is critical and necessary for the attainment of both (a) and (b). Harold Cruse, in his work *Plural But Equal*, has commented on how Black self-help has been impossible without concomitant Black political mobilization. He points out, furthermore, that historically Black self-help efforts have generated white political opposition in American society.[10] In fact, while both neo-conservatives and liberals bicker uselessly about Black self-help, there are ongoing institutional initiatives and programmatic efforts in Black urban communities across the United States that reflect all of the three components listed above.

This book is a collection of polemical essays by Black scholars and activists, some of whom focus on theoretical critiques of the current liberal and neo-conservative public policy paradigms. Other authors in this collection describe concrete and programmatic efforts aimed at black economic and community development strategies that do not easily fall into liberal or neo-conservative categories. The major purpose of these essays is to broaden the public policy and activist debates that have emerged in the last several years regarding the growth and persistence of negative living conditions in the Black communities of urban America. The essays represent an attempt to provoke thought about philosophical and political direction, rather than presenting empirical evidence for a particular hypothesis about Black community and economic development.

One important theme of this collection is that when considering race and public policy the Black "individual" or Black "family" should not be the only, or even primary, unit of analysis. Rather, considering the Black *community* as a whole encourages different approaches to the social and economic problems facing Blacks in America. Thus, when liberal and neo-conservative scholars debate whether "vouchers" will help the Black individual or family with housing, they overlook what might be the impact of this kind of policy approach on the overall status of the Black community.

Yet another theme contained in this anthology is that the role of politics, as well as the distribution of wealth and power in society, are critically important factors in analyzing public policy and in suggesting the adequate responses to Black economic and social dislocation. The problem of poverty and the human suffering caused by unemployment and economic dislocation are primarily political phenomena, rather than processes that reflect individual or group inadequacy.

Social and economic conditions in certain sectors of the Black community are worsening, and public policy – whether controlled and administered by liberals or by conservatives – has not responded satisfactorily to deteriorating living conditions. Theories of cultural or human capital deficits as explanations of the lack of Black social and economic mobility are rejected as unfounded by the contributors to this volume. The human service and educational crisis of Black communities reflects systematic rather than individual or group cultural deficiencies.

Some of the essays, however, do focus on the need for a cultural renaissance, a raising of racial consciousness as a critical component of community and economic development. This approach to culture is different from that of liberal or neo-conservative scholars. The latter refer to economically dominant white, middle-class norms of cultural behavior; but for many Black activists and scholars cultural consciousness is enlarged to refer to the importance of acknowledging and appreciating the social and historical roots of the Black community in the US as part of a worldwide African diaspora.

Political mobilization is a requisite condition for improving significantly the quality of social and economic life in the Black community. All the essays suggest directly or indirectly that without political mobilization and community consciousness the social and economic problems of Black America will continue to worsen. The Black community must become more involved, therefore, in policy discussions and debates at all levels of government – and within the private sector – regarding broad and specific social and economic development. The absence of this kind of input will continue to produce misguided and ineffective liberal or conservative-oriented policy responses to the social and economic problems of Black urban communities. Collectively the essays suggest directions and concrete examples that might be considered as Blacks seek to enhance their level of influence in public policy.

The contributors include those who have studied theoretical issues about race, politics and economic power in American society over the last several decades, two mayors of major cities, and also experienced practitioners of government and economic development initiatives in Black urban communities. Special attention is paid to the ideological arguments of Black neo-conservative and liberal thinkers since they have officially and academically limited the conceptual boundaries and paradigms of public policy and social welfare for the Black community. Not all the policy areas and topics that could be examined are raised in this collection of essays. Taken together, however, they do paint broadly the theoretical and conceptual weaknesses of liberal and neo-conservative thinking and policy approaches regarding Black economic and social development.

The first two chapters critique aspects of both the economic and social development paradigms proposed for Black urban communities in the US by neo-conservative and liberal writers. Jeremiah Cotton, an economist, argues in Chapter 1 that the building of an independent Black political base must necessarily accompany any strategies for Black economic and community development. He calls for the building of an independent political party as a way of formulating relevant and effective strategies for Black economic development. In the following chapter Julianne Malveaux, a political economist, takes issue with those liberal and neo-conservative writers who have utilized "human capital" approaches for analyzing Black economic development and the role of women. The author illustrates substantial contrasts between the economic experiences of Black and white women, suggesting important differences in the kind of political programs necessary to address their respective needs. She argues, furthermore, that the political well-being of Black women is intricately tied to that of the Black male, Black family and Black community.

Chapters 3 and 4 focus on a favourite topic of both neo-conservatives and liberals: the so-called Black underclass. Chapter 3 by Mack Jones, a political scientist, illustrates how the emergence of the Black underclass is a direct consequence of national public policies and politics rather than character flaws found in Black individuals. Jones concludes that political mobilization is required before the social and economic problems of the Black or Latino underclass are alleviated in America. In Chapter 4 Charles P. Henry, another political scientist, illustrates how the weaknesses of the current literature and research inhibit effective policy, political and cultural responses to the problems of the underclass.

The next chapter by the editor, an educator and activist in the Boston area, shows that a human service crisis is indeed facing the Black community – as neo-conservatives and liberals have contended – but the only effective response to this crisis is a political one. The social and economic crisis in the Black community was specifically generated in recent years by political decisions on the part of the federal government. The human service crisis in the Black community is not moral or cultural, or a result of the so-called breakdown of the Black family as argued by both some liberals and neo-conservatives. The author proposes, as do others in the earlier chapters, that the Black community must become more highly politicized and progressive in order to respond effectively to this crisis. While neo-conservatives are generally correct in emphasizing that more money will not eliminate negative living conditions for Blacks, James Jennings would add that without a progressive grassroots-level political mobilization – especially of alienated sectors in the Black community – economic and social conditions will continue to worsen.

Chapter 6 by Walter Stafford, a professor of social welfare and public policy, adds a concrete example to the discussion by Jennings by examining the results of neo-conservative politics and public policies in New York City. He suggests that this city has been ruled by neo-conservative philosophy since its last major fiscal crisis in the mid seventies; the author examines the consequences of neo-conservative public policy on the quality of Black life. These policies certainly did not solve the social and economic problems facing the black community; in fact, they were responsible for worsening conditions. Stafford too calls for political mobilization as a response to a growing social, economic and educational crisis facing the Black community of New York City.

Chapter 7 is by labor historian and activist William Fletcher and a former Black mayor of Berkeley, California, Eugene G. Newport. In this essay the need for a "Black Agenda" or a philosophical vision challenging ideological assumptions of the liberal and neo-conservative schools is proposed. But Fletcher and Newport not only raise ideological concerns with these schools of thought, they also suggest a concrete and programmatic initiative that could take place in Black urban America. They contend that this new agenda must include the political mobilization of the Black community around progressive goals that expand the democratic rights of citizens, and challenge the particular distribution of wealth and its accompanying benefits.

In the next chapter Sheila Ards, a policy analyst, focuses on housing as a critical factor in any strategy for economic and social development in the Black community. She takes issue with those who would advocate a "voucherization" of housing services for the Black community. Instead she calls for the development of programs emphasizing community control over land development as the best alternative for Black economic development and increasing the amount of affordable housing.

In Chapter 9 a professor of social welfare and former activist with the National Welfare Rights Organization, Jacqueline Pope, reminds the reader of how public welfare bureaucracies confine the social and political growth of the Black community. This reflects the writing of progressive scholars like Charles V. Hamilton, Ira Katznelson, Francis Fox Piven, Richard Cloward and others. But Pope goes further by offering some ways in which Blacks might begin to change the paternalistic nature of urban social welfare bureaucracies. According to Pope the political control of public service bureaucracies is a necessary condition – as was proposed by the activist community in the sixties – for the cultural and economic revitalization of the Black urban community. The author does not see public service bureaucracies as technocratically neutral or harmless but as part of the concrete problems that Blacks must overcome in order to realize social and economic development. Unlike the neo-conservatives, she rejects market-based responses to this problem; instead, she calls for political mobilization and a raising of community and cultural consciousness of grassroots sectors in order to control the behavior of public service bureaucracies.

In Chapter 10 Keith Jennings proposes that the crisis of Black youth unemployment is actually politically induced for the purpose of pacifying potential Black working-class activism. He shows how continuing high levels of youth unemployment are a result of national policies and politics in the pursuit of profits. He argues effectively that economic development under capitalism has marginalized Black youth, and therefore national policies are currently and structurally ineffective in solving the crisis in youth unemployment in Black communities.

Chapter 11, by the former long-time editor of the *Review of Black Political Economy*, Lloyd Hogan, proposes that the African-American community should tap a world-based political economy in order to develop effective economic survival programs in the US. But perhaps his more important point is that Blacks must develop a new set of Afrocentric values in determining strategies for improving the community's economy. Such values are not generally reflected in the writings of liberal scholars, and have been misused by neo-conservatives, who separate values like racial pride, self-sufficiency and family from the need to politically empower the Black community.

In the Conclusion of this book, the former mayor of Gary, Indiana, Richard Hatcher, summarizes some of the major points raised in the earlier chapters and discusses the need for a "Black Common Market." Such a venture would reflect and be built upon the themes expressed by the contributors. It would represent an initiative that again is neither liberal or conservative but reflects instead a Black community perspective.

Notes

1. William J. Wilson, *The Truly Disadvantaged* (Chicago: University of Chicago Press, 1987), pp. 4–8, 20.

2. Shelby Steele, *The Content of Our Character* (New York: St Martin's Press, 1990).

3. Adolph Reed, "The Underclass as Myth and Symbol: The Poverty of Discourse About Poverty," *Radical America* (Summer 1991).

4. See Edward C. Banfield, *The Unheavenly City Revisited* (Boston: Little, Brown and Co., 1973); and Thomas Sowell, *Civil Rights: Rhetoric and Reality* (New York: William Morrow Co., 1984); and Charles Murray, *Losing Ground* (New York: Basic Books, 1984).

5. See Oscar Lewis, *La Vida: A Puerto Rican Family in the Culture of Poverty* (New York: Random House, 1966); and Kenneth Auletta, *The Underclass* (New York: Random House, 1982).

6. See Kenneth M. Dolbeare *Democracy at Risk* (Chatham, NJ: Chatham House,

1986), and William R. Tabb and Larry Sawers, eds, *Marxism and the Metropolis* (New York: Oxford University Press, 1984); for a summary critique of this literature see James Jennings, "The Politics of Black Empowerment in Urban America" in Joseph M. Kling and Prudence S. Posner, eds, *Dilemmas of Activism* (Philadelphia, Pa.:Temple University Press, 1990).

7. See "The Uses of Linked-Development Policies in the US" in M. Parkinson, B. Foley and D. Judd, *Regenerating the Cities: The UK Crisis and the US Experience* (Glenview, Ill.: Scott, Foresman and Co., 1989); also see my critique in Kling and Posner, *Dilemmas of Activism.*

8. Parkinson, Foley and Judd, *Regenerating the Cities*, p. 94.

9. John Hope Franklin and Eleanor Holmes Norton, Committee on Policy for Racial Justice, "Black Initiative and Governmental Responsibility" (Washington DC: Joint Center for Political and Economic Studies, 1987), p. 40.

10. Harold Cruse, *Plural But Equal* (New York: William Morrow and Co., Inc., 1987), p. 294.

Towards a Theory and Strategy for Black Economic Development

Jeremiah Cotton

Black communities across the nation are largely concentrated in locales that share a common set of characteristics: a physically decaying residential and commercial infrastructure pockmarked with dilapidated and abandoned housing; boarded up storefronts; broken, littered sidewalks and trash-filled vacant lots. Most of the people living in these communities are beset by problems of poverty and near-poverty, high unemployment and underemployment, high crime rates, little political influence, and, therefore, inadequate municipal services and concern.

Many have likened the conditions that exist within most Black communities to those of an underdeveloped Third World country. And just as underdevelopment in the Third World is the direct result of the exploitation of Third World resources by Western capitalist countries who used the ill-gotten gains to underwrite the development and overdevelopment of their own societies, so it is with the underdevelopment of the Black community in the United States. This exploitation began with slavery – when the initial Black labor input into the American production process was stolen outright from Africa – and continues up to the present with subsequent generations of Black labor undervalued and underpaid. And while it is clear in some areas that the current absolute material conditions of Black people in the United States, even perhaps those among the poorest, do not compare with the desolation and destitution of a Sudan or Bangladesh, the Black community is still in a very real and measurable sense underdeveloped.

The noted Guyanese historian Walter Rodney defined "development" as "increased skill and capacity, greater freedom, creativity, self-discipline, responsibility and *material well-being*" (my emphasis). On the other hand, the concept of underdevelopment, Rodney argued, is a relative, comparative one. For inasmuch as all people have achieved some measure of development, then

> underdevelopment only makes sense as a means of comparing levels of development . . . It is possible to compare the economic conditions at two different periods for the same country and determine whether or not it had developed; and (more importantly) it is possible to compare the economies of any two countries at any given period in time.[1]

Although it does not capture all of the dimensions and consequences of underdevelopment, the traditional indicator used by economists to gauge and compare the relative states of economic development of the world's nations is per capita Gross National Product (GNP). This is the value of the output of goods and services produced annually in a given country divided by the total population of the country. Table 1 lists the per capita GNP of various countries.

Table 1   Per Capita GNP for Selected Countries, 1987

Country	US $
Switzerland	27,300
Japan	19,410
United States	18,570
West Germany	18,450
France	15,620
United Kingdom	11,730
Soviet Union	8,662
Poland	6,879
Iran	5,129
Turkey	1,235
Sudan	369
Bangladesh	163
Ethiopia	112
Mozambique	85

Source: Statistical Abstract of the United States, 110th Edition, Table 1446.

In 1987, the per capita GNP in the United States was $18,570, compared to $27,300 in Switzerland and $19,410 in Japan, the two countries whose per capita income exceeds that of the United States. In West Germany per capita GNP was $18,450; in France it was $15,620; in Great Britain $11,730; and $8,662 in the Soviet Union. By contrast the per capita GNP in Iran was $5,129; in Turkey it was $1,235; in Ethiopia $112; and in Mozambique just $85. The latter four countries are without question underdeveloped. Yet the degree of underdevelopment varied greatly between say, Iran and Ethiopia.

While there are no separate Black–white data on per capita GNP in the United States there are plenty of other comparative indicators of Black–white economic differences, or differences in their relative states of economic development. There are data, for example, on per capita *money* income.[2] Table 2 compares Black and white per capita money income at five-year intervals between 1969 and 1989.

Table 2   Black–White Per Capita Money Income, Selected Years (in 1989 dollars)

Year	Black per capita income ($)	White per capita income ($)	Black/white ratio	Black–white difference ($)
1969	5,205	9,668	0.56	4,463
1974	6,836	11,764	0.58	4,928
1979	7,590	12,936	0.59	5,346
1984	7,491	13,055	0.57	5,564
1989	8,747	14,896	0.59	6,149

Source: US Bureau of Census, *Current Population Reports,* "Money Income and Poverty Status in the United States, 1989," Series P-60, No. 168, Table 17.

In 1989, the per capita money income for whites was $14,896 and that for Blacks was $8,747, giving an absolute difference in respective incomes of $6,149. The relative difference, measured by the income ratio, means that for every $1 of white money income per capita, Blacks had 59 cents. And while the relative differences appear to have narrowed slightly between 1969 and 1989 (0.56 vs 0.59), the absolute differences sharply increased ($4,463 vs $6,149). An even more telling indicator of the relative economic situation of Blacks and whites is family wealth or net worth shown in Table 3.[3] In 1984, the net worth of the average white family was $46,706, while that of the average Black family was $4,054. This means that for every dollar in wealth held by a white family a corresponding Black family had just 9 cents. Indeed, the wealth disparity between Black and white families was so great that a white *female-headed* family had more average wealth than a Black *married couple* family ($26,853 vs $15,588).

The situation with respect to differences in Black–white capital and business assets ownership is even worse. In 1989, Blacks owned just over 2 per cent of all US capital assets. Among the top hundred Black businesses identified in 1979 by *Black Enterprise* magazine number one was a food processing and distribution company, TLC Beatrice International, with nearly $2 billion in sales in 1988. Number two was Johnson Publishers (*Ebony* and *Jet*), with nearly $210 million. Among Black banks the Seaway National Bank of Chicago had $150 million in

Table 3 Black–White Family Median Net Worth, 1984 (in 1989 dollars)

Net worth by income class	Black family net worth ($)	White family net worth ($)	Black/ white ratio
All income classes	4,054	46,706	0.09
Less than $10,000	105	10,076	0.01
$10,000 to $23,000	5,034	56,656	0.14
$24,000 to $47,000	19,068	60,304	0.32
$48,000 and over	70,125	153,045	0.46
Net worth by family type			
Married couple	15,588	64,666	0.24
Female-headed	801	26,853	0.03

Source: US Bureau of Census, *Current Population Reports,* "Household Wealth and Asset Ownership: 1984," Series P-70, No. 7, Table G.

assets and Freedom National Bank of New York, with no hint of the coming bankruptcy that would close it in 1991, had just under $120 million. As for insurance companies, North Carolina Mutual Life had nearly $9 billion worth of insurance policies and Golden State Mutual of Los Angeles had almost $5 billion.[4] Yet all major Black US corporations combined could have been bought out in 1989 with the liquid assets of just one or two of the top US corporations, such as Mobil Oil or General Electric.

Perhaps the most clear-cut indicator of the gulf between the economic fortunes of Blacks and whites in the United States is their respective poverty rates. As Table 4 reveals, poverty among both Blacks and whites fell during the fifteen-year period from 1959 to 1974, and rose over the next fifteen-year period, from 1974 to 1989. However, over the entire thirty-year interval, whether falling or rising, Black poverty has been three times greater than white poverty.

In 1989 the official poverty standard was set at an income of $12,675 for a non-farm family of four. This meant that 9.3 million of the country's 30.3 million Blacks were counted as poor on that basis compared to 30.8 million of the 207 million whites. Thus the Black rate of 30.7 per cent was over three times as great as the 10 per cent white rate.

But even the quality of Black and white poverty differs. While the majority of poor whites live in urban areas, unlike poor Blacks only a small percentage live in the blighted poverty enclaves of the inner cities. Most live outside in low-income suburban neighborhoods, or if they do live in the inner-city they live in declining yet fairly well serviced ethnic

Table 4   Black–White Poverty, Selected Years

Year	Poor blacks ('000)	Black poverty rate (%)	Poor whites ('000)	White poverty rate (%)	Black/ white ratio
1959	9,927	55.1	28,484	18.1	3.04
1969	7,095	32.2	16,659	9.5	3.39
1974	7,182	30.3	15,736	8.6	3.52
1979	8,050	31.0	17,214	9.0	3.44
1984	9,490	33.8	22,955	11.5	2.94
1989	9,305	30.7	20,788	10.0	3.07

Source: US Bureau of Census, *Current Population Reports,* "Money Income and Poverty Status in the United States, 1989," Series P-60, No. 168, Table 19.

neighborhoods. The white poor tend to pay less for their goods and services because many more retailers are located in their neighborhoods and hence they do not have to pay the transportation costs incurred by poor Blacks who must seek similar goods and services outside of their areas. Moreover, merchants in black communities tend to face higher insurance costs because of their higher perceived risks and therefore they charge the Blacks higher prices. Still more importantly, the routes out of poverty for whites are not dead-ended and detoured by racially discriminatory barriers, as they are for Blacks.

Due to the rhetoric of American democracy, as well as the lately acquired pretense of racial equality, the United States government has been forced at times to make some effort to address the long-standing crisis of Black underdevelopment. Typically most of these efforts have been half-hearted, piecemeal, inadequate and, of course, hugely unsuccessful. This is not surprising since their major purposes have not been, for the most part, Black community development but Black pacification.

The last great government maneuver in this regard was the "war on poverty" of the 1960s. It came into being in response to the pressure being put on the society by the mass protesting and rioting in Black communities. Despite the great to-do made, and in spite of the creation of bureaux and agencies and commissions and demonstration projects and grand designs, very little of any lasting material benefit to the Black community as a whole came out of the skirmish. The Black poverty rate in 1966, one of the years when the opening shots in the "war" were fired, was 33.4 per cent, and in 1989, as previously noted, it was 30.7 per cent. In 1967, for every $1 of income received by the average white family the average Black family had 59 cents. By 1989, a Black family had only 56 cents per every white family dollar. In 1965, the Black male unemployment rate was just over twice the rate of white males and the

Black female rate was just slightly less than twice the white female rate. By 1989, the Black male rate had grown to over two and three-fourths of the white male rate and the Black female rate was two and one-half times the white female rate.

Undeniably some segments of the Black community did gain from the events described above. A few Blacks moved into middle-class jobs and some moved out of the urban ghettos. However, the gains made by these Blacks have taken place in comparison with other Blacks, not in comparison to similarly placed whites. The earnings gap between Black and white workers in upper-level white-collar occupations such as doctors, lawyers, teachers, business executives and natural and social scientists is greater than that between Black and white blue-collar workers. In 1987, for every $1 earned on average by white males in upper-level white-collar occupations a similarly placed Black male earned 71 cents, and a Black female earned 51 cents. For every $1 earned by a white male blue-collar worker, his Black male and female counterpart earned 79 cents and 54 cents respectively.[5]

Despite the relative dearth of material benefits coming out of the "war on poverty" there were undoubtedly some symbolic benefits and lessons to be gained not so much from the "war" itself but from the events that brought it on – the agitations for Black civil and legal rights. The country was forced to adopt a stated if not practiced policy of racial disinterest and therefore was obliged to suppress many of its more overt discriminatory postures. In addition it confirmed that the most effective and perhaps the only way of getting this society's attention is through concerted, even threatening action. It also seemed to confirm another crucial truth: that if any meaningful economic and social vitalization is to take place in Black communities, development that benefits all and not just a handful of individuals, it will have to be conceptualized, initiated and implemented by Blacks themselves. It is to this first task, that of conceptualization, that the rest of this essay will attempt to make a contribution.

The need for something like a "theory" of Black economic development is predicated on the simple observation that any purposive action, if it is to succeed, must be preceded by some sort of systematic thought or rationale that justifies its undertaking. Once such an analytic framework has been formulated then a plan of action or strategy can be derived from the principles and insights of the analysis.

The outline of a theory of Black economic development enunciated here is based on two major, interrelated hypotheses or assumptions, one drawn from contemporary economic thinking and the other from an older school of thought whose views have been largely abandoned and in some cases scorned by all but a few modern economic theorists. The first assumption involves what is called "market failure," that is, the inability of so-called free markets to produce either the kinds of goods and services consumers need and desire, or the proper amounts of those goods and services it does produce. It is therefore necessary for and incumbent on government to intervene and correct such markets. It will be argued here that the black community has been particularly victimized by failures in markets for labor and capital as well as in product markets.[6]

The second major assumption owes a debt to the notion espoused by many prominent economists at the turn of the century, notably Alfred Marshall, A.C. Pigou and John Bates Clark, who believed that economics was the science of "material well-being" (see Rodney's definition of "development" above) and that one person's well-being could be measured objectively and compared with that of another person. Moreover, society's total well-being, or social welfare, could be increased by redistributing income from those who are materially well off to those who are not.[7]

Taken together the two assumptions imply that due to widespread effects of pervasive market failure, one person's material well-being will be affected by and depend upon that of others. On this basis it is maintained that the economic development and vitalization of the Black community is in the best interests not only of Blacks themselves but also of the whole society.

It is well recognized in mainstream economic theory that extremely restrictive conditions must be met in order for a free-market, capitalist economic system to function smoothly and efficiently, producing the maximum amounts of the goods and services desired by society at the minimum cost in terms of society's resources. These conditions are rarely, if ever, approached in the real world.

First of all, the economic arrangement known as "perfect competition" must reign in all markets. And one of the most important characteristics of perfect competition is that there are so many well-informed, sophisticated and highly mobile buyers and sellers in a given market that no single one has any control over the market price. That is to say, in particular, no one firm or small group of firms can profit by unilaterally either raising or lowering the price being charged by all of the other firms in the market. If, for example, a firm were to raise its price in hopes of increasing its profits, buyers would simply purchase the good or service from another firm whose price had not changed. If on the other hand the firm lowered its price hoping to win customers or market share from other firms in the industry, the other firms would instantly match the price decrease, driving the market price down to just what it costs to produce the good. Any further price decrease would of course bankrupt all concerned. Indeed, this is precisely the price that prevails in perfectly competitive markets, the price that just covers the cost of production. And this price is determined not by the actions of any single buyer or seller but by the interaction of all of the many buyers and sellers in the market.

Another very critical feature of perfect competition concerns the nature of the good or service itself. The good must be such that only the buyer can gain satisfaction from its consumption. For example, only the person who pays for and consumes a hamburger sandwich benefits from it. A flu shot, on the other hand, while it may benefit the person who pays for and receives it, also clearly benefits other people as well. Moreover, others cannot be excluded from the benefits of the flu shot even though they did not pay for it. The flu shot is said to have "spillover benefits." And insofar as the price of a good or service represents the value consumers place on it as a consequence of the benefits they derive from its consumption, sellers will be reluctant to produce goods with spillover benefits because they cannot collect from the third parties who are enjoying the good but not paying for it. The markets in such goods will operate inefficiently because not enough of the goods will be produced.

Similarly, the seller is expected to assume all of the costs associated with the production of the goods it sells. Firms that pollute the environment in the process of manufacturing their products and who do not pay for the clean up or compensate those who are adversely affected by it are not bearing the full costs of their enterprise. They are instead shifting part of these costs onto others; these are known as "spillover costs," and when they exist too many of the goods will be produced.

In the cases of both the flu shot and the polluter, third parties who are not participants in the market either as buyers or sellers are helped or hurt by the market transactions. Whenever spillover benefits or costs occur markets fail to send the proper signals to buyers and particularly to sellers. Sellers either produce too little or too much of the good or service in question.

It should be noted in this context that there are some economic undertakings that create spillover benefits for some individuals or groups and spillover costs for others. A freeway built to run through or near a neighborhood might benefit those who use it by increasing their access to and exit from the city center. This might result in increased sales for downtown merchants. It might also, however, represent a significant cost to neighborhood residents who are either displaced or inconvenienced by the fumes, noise and debris from the freeway.

Market failure can also occur in markets for inputs into the productive process such as labor and capital. If, for example, there are only a few employers and many potential employees in a given labor market the employers will have a distinct advantage in negotiations over the price of labor (the wage) and over who does and does not get hired. On the other hand, if the workers band together and form a union or some other coalition they may end up with even greater market power than the employers or at least countervail the employer's power. Perfect competition, however, requires that neither employer nor workers have significant control over wages or hiring.

When market failure occurs, whether in markets for goods and services or markets for labor or capital, it is necessary for the government to intervene on behalf of consumers or other injured third parties and correct the markets. It can do so by regulating the behavior of those who have pricing power, or by requiring those who are benefiting but not paying to pay and thereby increase the output of the good, or by requiring those who are involved in harming others to cease and recompense their victims for past harm, and in so doing reduce the output of the good. It may also be necessary for the government itself to produce those goods that have significant spillover benefits. Goods such as flu shots, or education, or street lights, or police and fire protection are best produced in the public sector since the private sector will not produce a sufficient amount, being unable to capture all of the benefits that accrue from their consumption.

Now, of course, there are no markets in the real world that are perfectly competitive, and very few indeed that even come close to being so. Instead the United States economy is riddled with monopolistic and oligopolistic tendencies and elements. In and across virtually every major industry market power is concentrated in the hands of a relatively small network of economic actors who single-mindedly seek their own, usually short-run, ends. There are numerous structural and institutional barriers that prevent many workers both from obtaining labor market skills and selling what skills they have at wages commensurate with their value. Most consumers have very little accurate information about the relative prices and quality of goods and services or the availability of lower-priced substitutes. Spillover benefits and costs abound and are associated with the production of most goods and services that comprise the national output.

The theory of Black economic development therefore takes market failure and the necessity for government intervention in the economic affairs of the society as a starting point. Moreover, the fact that the current underdeveloped status of the Black community is due primarily to the structural inequities and failings of markets makes the economic well-being of this community especially tied to government interposition. In markets for consumer goods and services the Black community is generally overcharged and underserved. Blacks receive less and pay more for consumer credit that is used to purchase so many of the goods, particularly durable goods, in today's economy. The monopolies over well-paying jobs and career ladders in primary labor markets held by whites and their total and exclusive control of capital markets result in Blacks being underemployed, underpaid and undercapitalized. The Black community has also suffered enormous spillover costs, first from the abandonment of urban areas for suburban living by whites, taking with them a significant proportion of the taxes needed for the maintenance of schools, hospitals and the urban infrastructure. And Blacks also suffered from the replacement or appropriation of their neighborhoods to make way for the gentrified return to the city of economically mobile and upscale whites.

But even more importantly, with the huge potential social and economic returns or spillover benefits inherent in increased provision of goods and services to the Black community such as education, training, health care, adequate housing and community protection, it is "economically logical" for government to see to their provision as well as intervene in good and resource markets on behalf of the Black community. This results in a greater good for the entire society. Thus, government resources (and by extension those of the entire society) are critical – nay, indispensable – inputs in the development of the Black communities.

In contrast to the older definition of economics as the science of "material well-being," the modern definition is that economics is the science of "scarcity." The former is a group-oriented, cooperative concept; the latter carries the seeds of individualistic competition. What the older school thought of as material welfare, the modernists reinterpret and call "utility." Utility is believed to be a subjective condition and therefore not susceptible to either measurement or interpersonal comparison. All one can do is rank the order in which each individual derives relative amounts of utility from a given set of consumption activities. Each individual will have a unique, incomparable utility ranking or function – "one person's meat is another person's poison." Utility represents an individual's *preferences*, or *tastes*. Material well-being, on the other hand, is an objective condition and represents the individual's physical state or health – whether one is sufficiently fed or clothed, not whether one particularly "preferred" what was eaten or worn.

Thus, when the material well-being school spoke about being able to compare one person's material well-being with that of another person, they meant the "needs" of the two individuals. They focused on the ability of goods and services to satisfy material needs and on this point economists Robert Cooter and Peter Rappaport assert that "the comparison of needs, not the comparison of subjective desires, was what they [the material well-being theorists] meant by comparing utilities of different persons."[8] The material welfare theorists were fully aware of the difference between individual preferences and material well-being. But the former concept had not nearly so much social and economic significance as the latter. For the purposes of making policies affecting the lives of people, material well-being, defined as food, shelter, clothing, health care and the like, was the most relevant concept.

One of the major implications of interpersonal comparisons of material welfare or utility that modern theory most eschewed was the notion that a dollar of income received by a poor person would increase their material well-being by a greater amount than the same dollar received by a rich person; and therefore, society's or the group's total welfare could be increased by any income redistribution scheme that takes income away from those in the group whose material well-being would be reduced by *less* than the increase in well-being of those who received the income transfer. This assumes that a dollar of income is more valuable to a poor person than to a rich one. Moreover, to those who claimed that income redistribution would dampen the incentive to work and invest by those from whom income is taken, the material welfare adherents pointed out that the better fed, clothed and housed people are, the more productive and efficient they become, and this long-run increase in productivity and efficiency will more than offset any short-run losses resulting from an income redistribution.

But if both market failure with its spillover effects and the material welfare school are to be believed then not only is it possible to make interpersonal comparisons of material welfare or utility (to reclaim the concept from modern theory), but interdependency of material welfare also exists. That is to say, one person's material welfare is dependent not only on her or his individual consumption but on the consumption of others as well. It is precisely what is implied by spillover benefits and costs. If, for example, the benefit from one person's flu shot "spills over" onto another person then clearly the material welfare of the two individuals is intertwined.

This is a powerful, group-affirming notion that flies in the face of the social thinking developed in Western capitalist societies that has always stressed the primacy and transcendence of the individual over the group. Indeed, individuals by their very nature are perceived to be deeply antagonistic to the group. Human nature is viewed as selfish, highly competitive and essentially isolated. The group tends to stifle individual initiative and smother identity beneath layers of customs, norms and taboos. It impedes the individual's attempt to triumph over anonymity.

In economics the grand theme of individualism was first laid down by the eighteenth-century moral philosopher and so-called father of political economy, Adam Smith. He advocated a very limited role for government in the private economic affairs of the society. The mercantilist state that was slowly giving way to petty capitalism had operated on the ostensible assumption that the best way to benefit the entire society or group was through centralized control of its economic forces. It therefore kept both capital and labor under tight control, limiting the mobility of both by telling the former when, what and how much it could produce and the latter where, how and for whom it could work.

With the doctrine of *laissez faire* Smith supplied the logic in favor of the unfettering of these individual, productive forces. In his famous "invisible hand" analogy he argued that individuals acting in their own best, essentially selfish, interests will through the magic of the marketplace increase the total wealth and well-being of the entire nation:

> [An individual] generally, indeed, neither intends to promote the public interest, nor knows how much he is promoting it . . . He intends only his own gain, and he is in this, as in many other cases, led by an invisible hand to promote an end which was no part of his intention. Nor is it always the worst for the society that it was not part of it. By pursuing his own interest he frequently promotes that of the society more effectually than when he really intends to promote it.[9]

All of this was certainly in the best interests of capitalism because it was most comfortable when it was not required to respond to any imperative other than its own private quest for profits. It was also in capitalism's best interests for workers to act individually and not as a group, particularly when it came to negotiating wages.

Through Smith, selfishness, or (to cover it with a euphemism) self-interested behavior, was elevated to the level of a social good and the competitive struggle was blessed as a necessary test of survival and excellence. Modern theory therefore only had to take a short step back to its roots in Adam Smith to revivify the notion of individuality and replace the group-oriented concept of material well-being with that of "utility" as a subjective, private, immeasurable individual determination of well-being. And in this latter version since utilities are independent rather than interdependent individuals do not and need not necessarily derive any satisfaction, pleasure or benefit from the well-being of others, only from their own well-being. Thus, it is impossible to know whether a dollar will enhance the utility of a rich person less than that of a poor person because utilities are not comparable (the rich man could be a miser or hoarder of money whose only joy comes from adding another dollar to his wealth).

Individuality and independent well-being are the driving ideas behind capitalistic production, distribution and consumption. They permeate American economic psychology and certainly underlie both the often-voiced hostility toward people on welfare and others who cannot make it in the system, and the slavish admiration of the rich and famous. Moreover, the myth of the "loner" is a staple fantasy of Hollywood and television culture: John Wayne, Clint Eastwood or Rambo find it necessary to go it alone, outside of the group's laws, and often have to battle both the group and the group's enemies in order to save the group.

That this new theory of utility could replace the older, more trenchant notion of material welfare is an indication of the role modern orthodox economic theory was to assume for itself as apologist for the existing capitalist arrangements. These arrangements work best in an environment where "looking out for number one," predatory behavior is accepted and admired. Modern theory helped create that environment by apotheosizing the individual as the ideal unit of production and consumption.

There is no question as to which of these competing concepts is the more useful and relevant for defining the objective economic interests of the Black community. The ideas of interpersonal comparison and interdependency of material well-being or utility imply at one level that all Blacks are materially affected by the relative well-being of all other Blacks; and those who, for example, attempt to gauge Black economic progress by reference to the economic status of one segment of the Black community (such as the Black middle class, or particular professionals, businesspersons, athletes, or entertainers) are guilty of a kind of selectivity bias. It is not just the development and progress of a few, selected, individual Blacks or even particular sectors of the Black community, but the entire status and future of the Black community itself that is at issue.

At another level interdependent Black utilities or material well-being is the basis for what some have chosen to call "Black self-help," but is better realized as Black inter- and intracommunity cooperation, or "Black community help." For if each Black person's material well-being is dependent on that of all other Blacks then community co-operation rather than individualistic competition should prevail as an economic behavioral norm in the Black community. Black people have been largely undifferentiated in the white mind, treated as an inter-changeable, homogeneous other. That is enough in itself therefore to weld Black people together. For if all are ill-treated more or less alike then all have a common material interest in relief from and alteration of that treatment.

One reflection of the uniformity of Black ill-treatment is mirrored in the fact that as much or more of the 1987 Black–white earnings differences in upper-level white-collar occupations (the jobs held by the Black middle class) were due to "unexplained" causes as was that in blue-collar occupations. In dollar terms, only $1,821 of the $12,648 earnings difference between Black male and white male managers and professionals, and $2,706 of the $21,137 difference between Black female and white male managers and professionals, was due to human capital differences, that is, differences in education and work exper-ience, the major theoretical determinants of earnings (white males earned on average $43,130, Black males, $30,482; and black females, $21,993). This means that over $10,000 of the Black–white male, and $18,000 of the Black female–white male earnings differences were due to "other causes." A very strong candidate as an "other cause" is labor market discrimination. For Black and white male blue-collar workers, $352 of the $5,805 earnings difference, and $361 of the $12,903 Black female–white male earnings difference, was due to differences in educa-tion and work experience (white males earned $28,017; Black males earned $22,152; and Black females earned $15,114). As in the white-collar case, the rest of the earnings differences were "unexplained."

Thus, despite the current celebratory talk about the growth and affluence of the Black middle class and the declining significance of race as a barrier to their upward mobility, the operative word still appears to be "Black" not "class," middle or otherwise. Therefore it is clearly in the material self-interest of all Blacks, whatever their so-called class, to work actively and cooperatively for an end to the economic inequality of all other Blacks. A most important and urgently needed step toward that goal is the economic development of the Black community. And there are indeed active and significant roles for all segments of the Black community, including the Black middle class, to play in that development.

The twin policies of external assistance via the government's redistribution of resources and provision of social goods for the Black community and internal assistance in the form of Black community cooperation flow naturally from this model. Of course the adoption and implementation of such policies is another matter entirely and one that will require a range of strategies and tactics.

First, to put it quite bluntly, it must be clearly recognized that although government has both an economic and moral obligation to provide reconstruction resources to the Black community it will not do so unless absolutely forced to. The *actual*, or functional, role of government in a capitalist, racialist state is to serve as guardian and enforcer of the capitalist and racial hegemony. It is predisposed to, and responsive to, these interests and will take notice of other claims only if they appear to threaten them. Therefore massive political pressure must be put on government and through it on the rest of society to acknowledge and recompense the Black community for past and present underdevelopment caused by the malfunctioning, and in many instances malevolence, of this system.

As for the forms of this pressure, it must be recognized that decorous representations and entreaties to government by minor Black elected officials working through "appropriate channels" will not by themselves get the Black community very far. Neither should much be expected from the polite agitations and admonitions of the so-called national Black establishment leadership. There will have to be an insistent and unrelenting outcry from all segments of the Black community and it may well be necessary to mount mass demonstrations and civil disobedience on the order of those of the 1960s as part of this strategy.

One former civil rights activist stated "we struggled in the '50s to integrate the lunch counters and ballot boxes. And we've got to struggle in the 80s to integrate the money."[10] And he could have added that the struggle associated with the latter may be even more intense and require even more vigorous action than the former struggles did. Jesse Jackson's "street heat" will have to be translated into concrete social, political and economic actions. A society that can come to grips with its treatment of its Japanese-American citizens during World War II and compensate them for the injustices done can also be made to face up to the still unpaid claims of its African-American citizens. It must not be supposed that this acknowledgement by the government of its debt to the erstwhile Japanese-American internees was brought on by some sudden fit of moral compunction. Not a bit of it. Rather, it had everything to do with the considerable economic power wielded in world and US markets by Japan. It was not an act of contrition but one of economic self-interest. The government must be made to recognize that it is in the country's self-interest to address the unfinished business of the long-standing injustices to the Black community as well.

One form of economic pressure might require a return to the early boycotts, such as that of the Montgomery bus company, that helped kick off the civil rights movement. The Black community had roughly $220 billion in income at its disposal in 1971, and of course most of it was spent with white-owned and operated corporations and industries. Many of these businesses depend quite heavily on the Black billions for their survival. The businesses that benefit from Black expenditures must be made to join in the chorus of Black demands – it is, after all, in their economic interests as well.

Politically, Jesse Jackson and the Rainbow Coalition notwithstanding, the Black community must undertake a thoughtful reconsideration of its current political allegiances and affiliations and seriously contemplate the formation of a Black-led independent political party. Neither of the two major political parties are vehicles for the type of economic policies and changes required to bring about the vitalization of the Black community. One might perhaps occasionally find a more sympathetic ear or hear a more sympathetic rhetoric among the Democrats than among Republicans, but by and large they share the same material unresponsiveness to Black well-being.

A Black independent political party whose principal platform is the reconstruction of the Black community could and would have a very profound effect on Black people and other progressive political elements. It would no doubt shake up and rearrange the current political landscape to a degree as yet unimagined. It has the potential of bringing Blacks to the polls in unprecedented numbers – an event dreaded in the past by Republican and Democrat alike. And, rather than having their votes already counted in the columns of one party and ignored by the other, a genuine parley would have to take place in order for either party to win (temporary) Black support. But rather than throwing their weight behind candidates from either of the other two parties, a Black independent party could conceivably elect its own and other progressive candidates, particularly to local and state offices where the political decisions are made that most affect a community's life.

So far little or nothing has been said about the specific extent, thrust or forms of government intervention. Contemplating the problem in 1979, economists Sue Marshall and David Swinton placed the income deficit in the Black community at a minimum of $50 billion and the job deficit at 1.5 million jobs.[11] This not only gives a lower-bound estimate of the magnitude of the reconstruction task but also points out the necessity for "people-" as well as "place-oriented" development goals.

Black economic development must be concerned with the development of human as well as physical capital. Job creation, as economist Robert S. Browne indicated, must be at the top of the development agenda:

> The provision of adequate employment is clearly the *sine qua non* of any community revitalization program. One could expend vast sums on the physical renovation of neighborhoods – on repaving of streets and curbs, renovation of housing, planting of grass, trees, and shrubbery, more frequent garbage removal, better police work – and still discover that the community remains depressed and dispirited so long as widespread unemployment persisted.

Although the converse is not necessarily true, that is,

> the presence of full employment in a community will not guarantee that the community will be free of many negative characteristics; a fully employed community is not only less likely to suffer major deterioration than a largely unemployed one but also is better able to take self-improvement initiatives on its own or with a minimum of outside assistance.

It should further be specified that the employment created must not be entirely of the low-wage, service or secondary sector variety. Many good-paying jobs both in the private and public sector could be created by the desperately needed rebuilding of the national infrastructure of roads, highways, bridges, schools, and the clean up of the land and water pollution that is choking the social and economic arteries. This really is the real national defense and the value of these tasks and their spillover benefits are well-nigh immeasurable and worth paying top money to have performed.

A capital transfer or redistribution, of the order of that envisioned as a result of the coming bailout of the savings and loan industry, will be needed to begin the repair and physical improvement of the principal areas in which the Black community resides. It is conservatively estimated that $150 to $200 billion will be made available to the S&Ls over the next ten years. Surely if it is in the national interest to bail out an industry whose bankruptcy is largely the result of its own malpractices, it is in the national interest to improve the conditions of the 12 to 15 per cent of the population who, ironically enough, have never been very well served by the lending practices of the savings and loan industry.

The management and disbursement of these capital funds would of course be a massive undertaking and to handle the tasks many mechanisms, agencies and corporations would have to be established and coordinated both within and outside of the Black community. Care would have to be taken to make sure that all of the layers of decision-making and implementation generated are legitimated by, and responsive and accountable to, the Black communities on whose behalf they act.

In order to reconstruct and vitalize Black communities a considerable amount of what might be called "external capital" will be needed – that is, capital emanating from outside the Black community. Much of this capital, it has been argued above, should come from government either as compensation for spillover costs incurred by the Black community resulting from long-term, systematic market failures, or as an investment in the social good of Black improvement whose immense spillover benefits will redound to the entire society. There will also be a need to generate what could be called "internal capital," but is perhaps better termed Black community capital. This is very different from Black capitalism. The latter is at best a piecemeal or trickle-down solution when what is needed is not top–down development but bottom–up; at worst it is a replacement of a white with a Black form of exploitation.

The generation of Black community capital entails both physical, commercial and human capital development. And while, as previously noted, human capital in the modern parlance focuses on the acquisition of education and training, for the Black community it is even more basic. It begins with the feeding and housing of the Black hungry and homeless and making particularly certain that Black infants and children receive proper nourishment. It is, after all, absurd to expect tired, ill-clad, ill-nourished children to be motivated and perform well in school, or even to care about school at all. This is certainly one of the tasks that the Black middle class can undertake – ensuring the feeding, clothing and sheltering of poor Black children.

Historically, both Father Divine and more recently the Black Panthers made the feeding of the poor, and especially poor children, a cornerstone activity. Surely the Black middle class can do no less. This is an even higher priority and unambiguous undertaking than acting as "symbols" and "role models" and attempting to change the values and attitudes of the so-called "Black underclass" through persuasion and remonstrance, as seems to have been recommended by some Black and white critics of the Black community's self-help efforts. The marshaling of food and housing for the Black poor is to see to their material, rather than moral, well-being. It would be both a developmental and a revolutionary act.

A number of Black analysts have suggested another important development task that could be spearheaded by the Black middle class. A fairly substantial amount of community-owned capital for equity investments in Black enterprises could be raised from their savings (and from the savings of the working class as well, it might be added). A corporation could be set up and shares sold that have a guaranteed face value and rate of return. The government could act as the guarantor of both the principal and the yield and encourage purchases of the shares by exempting the yield from taxes. The corporation fund could be leveraged many times its initial magnitude and provide an internally generated and controlled pool of finance capital.

The fund and ownership of its shares could have great symbolic value serving as an act of solidarity and identification with the plight of the Black community, and an investment in its efforts to bring about change. As an internal act of income redistribution, and in accord with the conclusions from the theory of material well-being that a dollar transferred from one who is relatively well-off to one who is less well-off increases the total material welfare of the group to which both belong, the Black middle class could buy and donate shares in the corporation to the Black poor and/or to community institutions and agencies who provide services to the Black poor.

Conclusion

The two central hypotheses of the theory of Black community economic development presented here place the onus for that development on the society and on the Black community itself. The government acting for the society must step in and commit resources to the rebuilding of the Black community much as it did for the rebuilding of Germany and Japan after World War II. And just as it was in its social, political and economic interest to restore the economies of those former enemies, even more so is it in its interest to do so for its own, in many ways incomprehensibly loyal, African-American citizens. Such a commitment and undertaking would go a very long way toward retiring the debt owed to Black people and ending the racial guilt and strife that still haunt this society.

Many people maintain – and rightfully – that the society is all the better now for having faced up in the 1960s and 1970s to the social and legal injustices inflicted on the Black community in the past and enacting laws to correct them. How much more better off would the society be if it now completed that task by addressing the effects of past and present economic injustices done to the Black community.

But just as the society had to be pushed into taking that first step toward restoring the civil and legal rights of Blacks, so it will no doubt have to be pushed to take the next step and repair the physical and economic damage. The Black community must therefore again mobilize a concerted and sustained protest against the conditions imposed on it by a society that has not yet come to terms with its obligations. The revival of the unfinished agenda might require different tactics this time. It may be necessary for the Black community to create its own political center rather than depend on the kindness of strangers in the Democratic and Republican parties. The American political and economic system, being composed primarily of monopoly and oligopoly elements, responds only to other centers of power. It simply ignores those who are fragmented and powerless.

The Black community must also therefore use its considerable buying power in a concentrated manner in order to influence the many markets that benefit from its flow but underserve the community. The reason for the Black community acting in an organized, unified way is precisely because of the strong interrelationship between the material well-being of one sector or segment of the Black community and all other sectors. By themselves, individually, these sectors are economically and politically weak and vulnerable; in concert they are, just as they were in the recent past, a formidable social and moral force. The spirit and daring of the civil rights movement must be revived and infused into the economic rights movement that is the next stage in the struggle.

Notes

1. Walter Rodney, *How Europe Underdeveloped Africa* (Washington, DC: Howard University Press, 1982), p. 14.

2. Money income is identified in the National Income Accounts as "Personal Income" and defined as GNP *minus* depreciation, business taxes, social security contributions, corporate and personal income taxes and undistributed corporate profits *plus* transfer payments such as social security and public assistance.

3. The census definition of net worth is "the value of interest-earning assets . . . stocks and mutual fund shares, residential and rental property, vacation homes and land holdings, a business or profession, mortgages held by sellers, and motor vehicles, *less* liabilities in the form of any debts secured by any asset, credit cards, store bills, bank loans or other unsecured debts."

4. "The Black Enterprise 100s: The Nation's Largest Black Businesses," *Black Enterprise*, vol. 19, no. 11 (June 1989), p. 185.

5. See Jeremiah Cotton, "The Gap at the Top: Relative Occupational Earnings Disadvantages of the Black Middle Class," *The Review of Black Political Economy*, vol. 18, no. 3 (Winter 1990), pp. 21–38.

6. See Robert Haveman, *The Economics of the Public Sector* (New York: John Wiley & Sons, 1976) for an excellent, non-technical discussion of perfect competition, market failure and the need for government intervention.

7. The entire discussion of the material welfare school undertaken in this essay is heavily indebted to the article by Robert Cooter and Peter Rappaport: "Were the Ordinalists Wrong About Welfare Economics?," *Journal of Economic Literature* 22 (June 1984): pp. 507–30.

8. Ibid., p. 516.

9. Adam Smith, *The Wealth of Nations* (New York: Random House, 1937), Book IV, Chapter 2, p. 423.

10. Andrew Young as quoted by Juan Williams in "The Black Elite," *The Washington Press Magazine* (January 4, 1981), p. 17, cited in William Darity, Jr., "The Goal of Racial Economic Equality: A Critique," *The Journal of Ethnic Studies* 10 (December 1981), p. 51.

11. Sue Marshal and David H. Swinton, "Federal Government Policy in Black Community Revitalization," *Review of Black Political Economy* 10 (Fall 1979), pp. 11–29.

12. Robert S. Browne, "Institution Building for Urban Revitalization," *Review of Black Political Economy* 10 (Fall 1979), p. 35.

2

The Political Economy of Black Women

Julianne Malveaux

The term "doubly disadvantaged" has been frequently used to describe the economic status, and especially the labor-market status, of Black women.* The double disadvantage consists of membership both in a minority group and in the gender that has the least economic power. But the term "double disadvantage" ignores yet another source of deprivation for the Black woman: the labor-market disadvantage experienced by her spouse, or by members of her family unit. Indeed, as Black male employment-population ratios have declined to below 60 per cent by 1984 (compared to white male employment-population ratios of more than 72 per cent), and as the number of Black females heading households has risen to more than 42 per cent, the family status of the Black woman may be perceived as a third labor-market disadvantage.

For many Black women the term "doubly disadvantaged" may also mean "doubly ignored." While the thrust of some academic research has expanded to include the needs of Blacks and of women separately, Black women too frequently "fall between the cracks" and are assumed to be addressed "someplace else." It is thus ironic for Black women to observe the rise of "women's scholarship" while noting that their own presence in this research is ignored. The irony is parallel to an irony white women expressed in their criticism of the "state of the art." Marianne Ferber, for example, referred to a tendency toward generalization when she noted that studies concerned only with men tended to

* This article was previously published in *The Year Left 2: Toward a Rainbow Socialism*, edited by Mike Davis, Manning Marable, Fred Pfeil, and Michael Sprinker (London: Verso, 1987).

be "globally" labeled, while those that referred to women stated so clearly.[1] She buttressed her case by citing articles with "global" titles (like "Work Roles and Earnings," and "Economics of Affirmative Action") that refer only to men. Similarly, my review of research on women in the workplace uncovered titles like "Women in Law," "Women and Work: Issues of the 1980's," and "Women, Work, and Wages." These articles or books refer briefly, if at all, to minority women. Hull, Scott, and Smith reinforce Ferber's point as it relates to Black women, entitling their book, "But Some of Us Are Brave: Black Women's Studies."[2]

The treatment of Black women in the academic literature on women in the workplace assumes that they, and by extension other women of color, are invisible. But the nearly six million Black women in the 1984 labor-force represented 12 per cent of the female labor-force; 2.6 million Hispanic women (or women of Spanish origin) represent 5 per cent of the labor-force. Although Bureau of Labor Statistics data do not report on the status of American Indian or Asian women, the recent influx of Vietnamese and Cambodians suggests that the labor-market presence of these women is rising as well. And so, though we are invisible in academic writing, women of color represent 20 per cent or more of the labor-force.

The problem is both a research question and a question of politics. From a policy perspective, the notion that "women" are similar in status strengthens the concept of a women's movement, lobby, or political base. Many researchers have accepted the premise that "all the women are white" and tend to gather data on that presumption. For example, Catalyst in 1980 gathered data on 816 two-career couples, but did not code their data by race.[3] Similarly, Ann Harlan (1982) studied women who received their MBA from Harvard University.[4] She, too, failed to code for race.

Shirley Harkess has discussed the literature on women's occupational experiences in the 1970s and has uncovered several shortcomings in existing research.[5] She notes that "very, very few" researchers "choose as their focus the systematic analysis of minority women's occupational experiences." Yet the Harkess review seems to accept the premise that "all the women are white" when she non-critically reports the results of several studies that use large data sets, but do not report results by race. In particular, Harkess discusses Cynthia Epstein's 1981 book, *Women in Law*,[6] without observing the cursory treatment Epstein gives Black women attorneys. Epstein's treatment of Black women is particularly troubling because some of her earlier work had focused on the status of Black women professionals.[7] However, the Epstein discussion of women's participation in bar associations glaringly ignores the role of Black women in associations like the National Conference of Black Lawyers and the National Bar Association. Instead, Epstein scrupulously but exclusively discusses white women's participation in women's law groups and in alternative legal associations like the National Lawyers' Guild.

The Harkess review highlights several other flaws in research on women, especially as it ignores the position of minority women. She cites a 1982 Langwell study on physicians that describes "men" and "women" physicians, but ignores racial differences.[8] Similarly, Harkess cites several studies in which, although large samples of women were used, the status of minority women is given inadequate attention. These include a study of more than 10,000 Michigan teachers by DeTray and Greenberg, where race is mentioned, but where the authors choose, for the sake of "brevity," to concentrate on sex differences.[9] Given the history of Blacks in the teaching profession (elementary and secondary school teaching was one of the few professional occupations in which Blacks were employed before 1960), such further investigation would have been illuminating. Another study mentioned by Harkess deals with the labor supply of nurses (Link and Settle, 1979).[10] Using a sample of nearly 5,000 married registered nurses, Link and Settle find significant differences in the labor supply of whites versus non-whites. Although these results are reported with others in tabular form, the finding is neither further discussed nor interpreted in the body of the article.

The Missing Variable of Race

Researchers like Harkess aren't the only ones who paint a portrait of the diversity of women in only the broadest strokes, excluding issues of race whenever convenient. Numerous activists have used the "feminization of poverty" as a rallying cry, without understanding that this phenomenon may have diverse meanings for women depending upon their race. In 1966, one-third of white families in poverty were female-headed; so were 42 per cent of Black families in poverty. By 1982, 40 per cent of white families in poverty were female-headed, as were two-thirds of Black families.[11] This trend, first observed by sociologist Diana Pearce,[12] has been further substantiated, dissected, and discussed by feminist sociologists, economists and others.

The "feminization of poverty" has been more than a discussion about trends in poverty data. It has "generated the beginnings of a political movement to create a public voice for this new and fragile bond."[13] Women organizers have taken the data out of the census reports and into the streets through organizations like New York's Women's Economic Literacy Project or California's Women's Economic Agenda Project. The goal of these organizations has been to disseminate information about the position of women in the economy, as well as to "call women to action."[14] For example, the cover sheet of the Women's Economic Agenda Project "call to action" reads: "2 out of 3 adults in poverty are women. What if we were all to go to the polls?"

The "call to action" assumes a set of common gender interests among women. Wendy Sarvesy describes the women touched by the feminization of poverty as "seriously ill women who lose medical insurance coverage when their husbands die, single working mothers who use most of their paychecks for childcare, displaced homemakers who have no marketable skills, teenage mothers who must drop out of school, suburban housewives whose husbands leave the state and default on child support payments, mothers who try to combine part-time work with childrearing, women who must quit their jobs to take care of sick children and other family members." Sarvesy asserts that these women share a condition which "cuts across class, race, age and sexual preference." But her acknowledgment that the bond is fragile is important, for while gender may bind women together at some level, there are important differences among women that prevent the development of a "women's agenda."

Although the "feminization of poverty" is a trend, and the germ of a political movement, it is also a poignant reminder that some problems generate attention only when white people are involved. The proportion of Black women heading households in poverty has been, over the past fifteen years, higher than the proportion of white women now heading families in poverty. And organization around the "feminization of poverty" ignores the persistent poverty that plagues Black, Hispanic and Native-American communities, a poverty that has a disproportionate impact on minority women and children, as well as on minority men.

Are the economic interests of Black and white women similar? All the data show that the economic status of Black and white women is clearly distinct.[15] A discussion of the political economy of Black women cannot be sustained only by inspecting selected aspects of Black women's lives. Above all, the economic position of Black women cannot be understood in isolation from the general discrimination in employment practices and the overall economic situation of Blacks as a group. Those who have spoken most persistently about the "feminization of poverty" summarize the position in the following slogan: "A woman is a husband away from poverty." But Black women are poor, even with husbands, because of the institutional racism that bars many Black men from employment. Similarly, the projection that by the year 2000 all the poor will be women and children will prove true if genocide (or full employment) is planned for men of color, and other men who are chronically poor and structually unemployed.

Pamela Sparr writes: "By stressing what is uniquely female, proponents of that argument may leave a mistaken impression that sexism is the fundamental problem. They fail to examine thoroughly the nature of the capitalist economy, which requires and maintains an impoverished class of people."[16] To the extent that this impoverished class is Black, and to the extent that Black women see the survival of their community as important, a set of policy initiatives addressed solely to the "feminization of poverty" may have limited interest for Black women.

The Economic Decline of the Black Community

During the middle and late 1970s, economists began to examine Black economic progress and to discuss the improvement in their relative economic status.[17] At the root of their analysis lay an improvement in relative income (until 1975), an improvement in the occupational status of Blacks, and an improvement in Black educational access. Critics of these writers argued that the data were focused too heavily on wages and salaries, thus overstating the gains by excluding those with zero wages and salaries.[18]

Today with a decline in Black income as a percentage of white income, an increase in the amount of Black poverty, and a decline in the employment-population ratio of Black men, it is less easy to assert Black economic progress. Shulman states he would not describe progress as "dramatic," and rejects "reported" convergence because the non-employed are frequently excluded from the research that reports convergence.[19] Bates disaggregates the Black experience regionally and notes that Blacks in "Northeastern and Midwestern states are losing ground rapidly."[20]

Even as some of the 1960–75 gains are eroded, Bates notes several significant factors that have improved the Black economic position. These include Black educational gains, an improvement in the occupational status of young Blacks, penetration into jobs from which Blacks had previously been excluded, and a significant change in the occupational status of Black women (largely the result of the declining proportion of Black female private household workers). Bates further notes that a set of "perceptual factors" have led to the appearance of Black economic progress. These include an increase in the number of Black elected officials, alterations in media stereotypes, and the increased visibility of Black managers and other professionals.

The "perceptual facts" Bates mentions, while undoubtedly real, must nevertheless be used with caution. One of the most visible changes among Blacks in the past two decades has been their entry into professional, technical and managerial jobs. When this entry is viewed over time, however, it is clear that the pace of occupational gains was most rapid between 1964 and 1972. The rate of occupational improvement declined somewhat between 1972 and 1977, at the same time that the rate of white female occupational improvement was rising.[21]

While the improved educational status of Blacks has provided a ticket to upward occupational mobility, and while researchers have reported Black and white college graduates being hired at nearly identical incomes (Bates, 1984), Black college graduates find their educations do not prevent their being slotted differentially in the labor process. For example, while 13 per cent of white male college graduates over age twenty-five have incomes in excess of $50,000, fewer than 2 per cent of Black male college graduates have similar incomes.[22] Interviews with Black MBAs indicate that the most advantaged Blacks in the labor market still experience discrimination as they move up the hierarchical ladder in corporations.[23]

Despite occupational advancement, fewer than 20 per cent of Black men and women worked in white-collar occupations; in 1982, fewer than 9 per cent of all Blacks were college graduates. Those Blacks not employed in professional and managerial jobs can be described as either "those who are not highly educated, yet not below average in skill and years of schooling," and "those on the bottom, perhaps representing a semi-permanent lumpenproletariat."[24] Those with average skills experience cyclical employment, while those on the bottom face uncertain job prospects. There is some evidence that the size of the group of Blacks on the bottom is growing.

The economic progress of the Black community may have been impeded by lax enforcement of affirmative action policies, by reinterpretation of the Civil Rights Act by the Reagan Supreme Court, and by judicial decisions that have made it more difficult to prove discrimination (see EEOC v. IBM, 34 FEP 766). Given poverty, high unemployment rates, declining Black male participation in the labor-force, and a public policy shift that has reduced social programs, the economic condition of Blacks remains as precarious as ever.

The economic progress of Blacks as a group is central to a discussion of the political economy of Black women. This progress is troubling, especially when viewed in tandem with the "feminization of poverty" and a "women's agenda." As the economic position of the Black community has steadily worsened, attention to the needs of Blacks has waned in the national public policy arena. Some Blacks view efforts to place the "feminization of poverty" in the forefront as an attempt to shift attention from the plight of the Black community. Others view with suspicion the attempts by white women to become spokespersons for the poor. And, while Black women may benefit from programs designed to fight the "feminization of poverty," a program for the Black community must do more than focus on its women.

Although few have formally articulated a "women's agenda," one of the efforts of mainstream women's organizations has been to improve the representation of women in the professions, in managerial jobs, and in highly visible jobs in the public sector. Too frequently, an effort to secure a position for an individual generates little more than symbolic gain for a group. We need to know more about the benefits of having women or Blacks on corporate boards of directors, in visible jobs, and in power. Do Blacks or women tend to hire more Blacks or women? Are women who gain jobs as a result of public pressure more likely to open doors for Blacks? If they are, it may be in the interest of Blacks to support a "women's agenda." If not, Blacks have little to gain by casting their lot with a progressive group whose values are color-blind.

Blacks have experienced both discrimination and economic disadvantage, while women have, in general, experienced discrimination but no more economic disadvantage than the men of their race and class. Since white middle-class women are the mothers, daughters, sisters and wives of white middle-class men, Blacks need to know whether these women will support their class interests or a broader set of interests as they enter public life and seek highly visible policy jobs. The answer becomes more critical as the position of the Black community in the national economy manifestly deteriorates.

Black Women in the Labor Market

Those who have attempted to use the "feminization of poverty" trend as a tool for political organizing have tended to blur differences between women of color and white women as they organize. They find support for their work from research that speaks about the "convergence" in the status of Black and white women.

Income data give some credence to the "convergence" argument. In 1984, the median wage for full-time women workers was $259 per week; it was $264 (or $13,700 annually) for full-time white women and $242 ($12,600 annually) for full-time Black women. Full-time Black women's earnings were 92 per cent of full-time white women's earnings. Given the comparatively small disparity, does it make sense to talk about the labor-market status of Black women as distinct from the status of other women? Some researchers think not, especially since Black women left private household work in large numbers between 1960 and 1970 to clerical jobs that had been dominated by white women. According to Bates, Black female income rose from 62 per cent of white women's income in 1960 to 96 per cent of white women's income in 1980.[25]

But raw income data only partially reveal the labor-market status of Black women. Black women participate in the labor-force slightly more than do white women, with the December 1985 labor-force participation of adult Black women at 59.2 per cent, while white female labor-force participation was 54.4 per cent.

The labor-force participation of young Black women has been dropping for some time, with participation rates for those in the 16–24-year-old group below 30 per cent in 1984. Barbara Jones cites the declining employment opportunities and increased competition for unskilled jobs as part of the reason labor-force participation rates for young women are so low.[26] The paucity of affordable childcare and job training may be other factors in producing these participation rates.

Further, Black women are more likely to work full-time than are white women; when they work part-time, it is more likely to be for economic reasons than is the case in white women's working part-time.[27] At every educational level, Black women more often work full-time than white women. Thus the "parity" in income levels that has been reported misrepresents the economic condition of Black women, since they reached this level only by working more than white women.

Black women have consistently experienced more unemployment than have white or Hispanic women, with Black women's unemployment levels tending to be twice those of white women. In December 1985, for example, the unemployment rate for adult white women was 5.4 per cent, while for adult Black women it was 12.6 per cent. Black women also lose their jobs more quickly than do white women during recessions. They also find jobs more slowly than Black men, white men and white women in periods of economic recovery. Black women's unemployment rates have shown less cyclical sensitivity than the rates of Black and white men, while improvement during recoveries is more highly correlated with the length of the recovery than is true of other race-sex groups.[28]

Perhaps the greatest difference in the status of Black and white women is in occupational status. At first glance, Black and white women seem to be distributed similarly in occupations. A third of all white women are clerical workers, as are 30 per cent of all Black women workers. Twenty-three per cent of all Black women work in service jobs, as do 16 per cent of white women. Fifteen per cent of Black women workers, and 17 per cent of white women workers, are employed in professional jobs.

However, Black women's occupational similarity to white women is less indicative of economic parity than of the impact of sex stratification on occupational attainment. While the gap between Black and white women's occupational status at the two digit level is narrower than that between Black men and white men, there are clear parallels between Black male and Black female occupational status. Black men are far less heavily represented in white-collar and skilled blue-collar jobs than are white men (for example, Black male professional, managerial, sales and crafts workers represent 38 per cent of all Black male workers, compared to almost 60 per cent of all white male workers). Similarly, a greater number of Black women work in non-white-collar (though mostly traditionally female) jobs than do white women. About half of all Black women work as operatives, private household workers, and service workers, while just 27 per cent of all white women work in those occupations. Black women also experience occupational segregation distinct from the occupational segregation white women experience. In addition to being employed in jobs that are "typically female," Black women are also employed in jobs that are "typically" or disproportionately *Black* female. If Black women are either deliberately or traditionally "crowded" into a few low-paying jobs, they lower average wages in those jobs where they cluster, and reduce competition (or increase wages) in the jobs where they are excluded. This concept of Black women's crowding explains, in part, why Black women receive lower pay than white women in similar occupations.

"Typical Black female" occupations are defined as those where Black women's representation is more than twice their representation in the labor-force. In service jobs, for example, Black women are over-represented by a factor of three or four as chambermaids, welfare service aides, cleaners and nurse's aides. Forty-one per cent of the Black women who work in service occupations are employed in these four jobs.[29]

Black women are also over-represented among childcare workers, whose full-time wage places them below the poverty line; food-counter workers, who earn similarly low wages; cooks, whose wages are also below the poverty line; and hairdressers. In fact, 83.3 per cent of the Black women in service occupations work in jobs defined as being crowded by Black women.[30] Sixty-nine per cent of all Black women in service jobs both experienced crowding and were employed in jobs where women's full-time, full-year pay, at less than $180 per week, was below the poverty level. (By comparison, 54.2 per cent of white women service workers, a proportionally lower number, held "typically Black female" service jobs and had low pay.) Another 8.2 per cent of Black women service workers employed in "traditionally Black female" jobs earned weekly pay that, on a full-time, full-year basis, placed them at less than 125 per cent of the poverty line. (For white women, the comparable number was 1.7 per cent.)

An examination of the data reveals further differences between Black and white women's occupational patterns. While white women are over-represented as dental assistants, Black women are just proportionately represented in this occupation. Full-time pay for dental assistants is higher than that of nursing aides, a job where Black women are heavily over-represented. Similarly, Black women are just proportionately represented as waiters, while white women are heavily over-represented in this occupation. While pay in the food service industry is low, there are reasons this job may be attractive to Black women. Here, discrimination and entry barriers must be considered.

A similar analysis can be done for Black women in three-digit clerical occupations. Clerical work employs both the largest number and the largest proportion of Black and white women. The 1981 median clerical wage of $219 places the average clerical worker out of poverty, but in the "near poor" category. Yet, the range of clerical pay is broad: postal clerks have median earnings of $382 per week, or almost $20,000 per year, while cashiers have median weekly pay of $133 per week, or less than $7000 per year. Interestingly, both of these occupations are considered "typical Black female" jobs.

As with service work, an examination of detailed clerical occupations reveals those enclaves that have become "typical Black female." Nearly a quarter of all Black women are concentrated in just six of forty-eight clerical occupations. They are over-represented by a factor of four as file clerks, typists, keypunch operators, teaching assistants, calculating machine operators, and social welfare clerical assistants.

Except for the median wage of social welfare clerical assistants, all of these occupations have median wages associated with the near poor. Those occupations in which Black women are most heavily represented have pay levels at 125 per cent of the poverty level or lower.

Nearly 60 per cent of Black women clericals work in "typical Black female" occupations, as do 40 per cent of female white clericals. Most of these Black women had wages at or below the near poor level. Nearly one in seven (13.7 per cent) of Black female clericals work in "typical Black female" jobs that pay at the poverty line or lower. Another 31 per cent of Black women clericals are both crowded into Black female occupational enclaves and among the working poor. A lower but sizeable number of white women share the characteristic of working in "typical Black female" jobs with low earnings.

It is important to note that nearly a third of Black women clericals were employed by government.[31] For many Black women, the fiscal health of federal, state and local governments affects wage levels. Further, layoffs of government workers may have a greater impact on Black women clericals than on others, both because of their heavy representation among government employees and because of the fact that many of them are recently hired municipal employees.

Aspects of Black women's crowding and concentrations of low wage workers in other occupations have been reviewed in earlier work by this researcher.[32] At the two-digit level, Black women are more concentrated in "blue-collar" typically female jobs than are white women; at the three-digit level, Black women are segregated into "typical Black female" enclaves where wages are lower than those for white women.

One must also give weight to an important historical dimension of the status of Black women in the labor market. Prior to 1940, the majority (60 per cent) of Black women worked as private household workers. A third of all Black women were still so employed in 1960, but just 6 per cent of all Black women worked in private households jobs in 1980. Partly because of this labor-market legacy, Black women have experienced as much, or more, occupational segregation as white women, but in a different set of jobs. Even as Black women's occupational patterns shifted between 1960 and 1980, Black women continued to be more heavily represented in "traditionally female" jobs than white women, and were more likely to work in service than in clerical jobs until quite recently.

Since 1970, all women have reduced their representation in "typically female" jobs. The reduction in the representation of Black women in these jobs reversed itself after 1977, while the representation of white women in such jobs has continued to decline. White women experienced less stratification from the outset, and have left segregated jobs more rapidly than have Black women. While the quality of work among Black women changed, it did so largely because they moved from one set of stratified jobs to another, not because they left "typically female" jobs.

There is also an age dimension to women's occupational segregation. While white women (especially those under thirty-five) are reducing their representation in "typically female" jobs, Black women in the same age group are increasing their representation in these jobs. The increase in Black women's representation in white-collar, "typically female" jobs among 25–34-year-olds means that Black women in that age group tend proportionally to be more heavily represented as clerical workers than white women in the same age group.

Occupational differences between Black and white women may mean these women have different labor-market interests and may choose different strategies for improving their status. Because of their high concentration in clerical jobs, white women may target these jobs for their organizing efforts. Although there is also a high concentration of Black women in clerical jobs, the second largest concentration is in service jobs; these jobs may be the target of Black women's organizing efforts. Trends in service work like the privatization of public services will also impact differently on Black women than on white.

The occupational differences between Black and white women can also produce open conflicts of interests. For example, some hospitals have begun to phase out nurse's aides to "professionalize" nursing services. Registered nurses have supported, and in some cases initiated, these changes. Black women are disproportionately represented as nurse's aides. A purely "women's agenda' offers few guidelines for balancing the job security of nurse's aides with the demand for "professionalization" by registered nurses.

"Feminization of Poverty"? Facts and Fiction

Earlier discussion in this paper referred to the "feminization of poverty" movement. It is helpful, given the discussion of the labor-market status of Black women, to review poverty trends to see whether the sweeping "feminization of poverty" to which activists refer has actually taken place. Between 1966 and 1973, poverty declined among individuals and families. The Black poverty rate reached its lowest point in 1974, when it was 30.3 per cent. This represented a decline of 27 per cent from its 1966 rate of 41.8 per cent. Among whites, poverty rates reached a low point in 1973, when 8.4 per cent of white families were at or below the poverty line.

Although poverty declined during the late 1960s and early 1970s there has been an increase in poverty in the past decade. The number of Black families in poverty has risen by 35 per cent since Black poverty rates reached their low point in 1974, an increase of 17 per cent. The rate of increase was highest from 1979 to 1982, when the number of Blacks in poverty rose by about half a million each year.

Trends in poverty among whites were similar to trends among Blacks. The number of whites in poverty has increased by 55 per cent since white poverty rates reached their low point in 1973. The white poverty rate fluctuated in the 1974–79 period, then increased. In each year between 1979 and 1982, roughly two million whites entered poverty.

The "feminization of poverty" was indeed an important part of these increases. Since 1966, the number of Black female-headed families has increased by more than 78 per cent, while the number of white female-headed families increased by about 44 per cent. The poverty rate for both Black and white female-headed families dropped between 1966 and 1982, but while rates fell between 1966 and 1979, they rose by 10 per cent for Black women between 1979 and 1982 and by 17 per cent for white women.

However, the increase in the poverty rate of female-headed families in the 1979–82 period has been accompanied by a decline in the percentage of poor families that are headed by women. Families headed by women accounted for more than 70 per cent of the Black families in poverty in 1978. This number had dropped to 67 per cent by 1982. Similarly, although white women headed almost 45 per cent of the white families in poverty in 1978, they headed 40 per cent of the white families in poverty in 1982.

While the "feminization of poverty" is important, there are other trends in the poverty status of Blacks and whites that must be considered. For instance, more men have fallen into poverty in recent years. While some male poverty is the short-term result of the 1981–83 recession, others have suffered the long-term consequences of shifts in the structure of the US economy. During the past fifteen years, Black male labor-force participation rates have dropped dramatically. They are now ten percentage points lower than the rates of whites (Bureau of Labor Statistics, 1984a). Timothy Bates (1984) has shown the substantial deterioration in the labor-market status of young (20–24) Black men, noting that their low labor-force participation rates may negatively affect their chances for future employment.

While all blue-collar workers, especially those in the auto, steel and other manufacturing industries, will experience negative effects from the deindustrialization of the American economy, there is evidence that Black workers, especially male, will have a longer recovery period than whites. A report on the status of workers who lost or left a job between 1979 and 1984 because of plant closures, slack work, or the abolition of their positions notes that 63 per cent of white workers have been re-employed, compared to 42 per cent of Blacks. More Black than white workers left the labor-force after they had lost their jobs.[33] Although there may be differences in the characteristics of Black and white workers that explain their different rates of re-employment, job tenure was not one of them. Black male workers who are displaced had longer job tenure than did their white male counterparts.

Data about the re-employment of displaced workers merely re-inforces the notion that Blacks fare disproportionately worse in the economy and are disproportionately affected by recession. A 1982 comparison of the effects of recession and recovery on Black workers noted that they had begun to experience larger increases in unemploy-ment rates during recessions, but smaller decreases during recovery.[34] Between September 1983 and September 1984, a period of "recovery," the ratio of Black–white male unemployment rates grew from 2.2 to 2.4.[35] The Black–white female unemployment ratio dropped from 2.4 to 2.2 during the same period, indicating a short-term improvement in the Black woman's employment position, but also indicating a long-term erosion in the relative unemployment rate of Black women, since the ratio before 1980 had never reached 2.

The causes of Black poverty are several. Too many Black women receive low pay and suffer uncertain employment while heading fami-lies. Young Black men and women have historically had a difficult time entering the labor market, while the labor market position of Black men has eroded in the past several years. The latter condition is illustrated by the decrease in the Black–white male unemployment ratio, in the decline in Black male labor-force participation, and in the increase in Black poverty that is less marked in female-headed households.

None of the facts about male poverty reduce the importance of poverty among women and children. However, an agenda that focuses solely on the "feminization of poverty" may not remedy the real causes of poverty in the Black community. Nor does it consider that the paths to poverty are several. Some people are poor because they are divorced; others are poor because they lack marketable skills; still others are poor because they face systematic institutional racism in labor markets. It is not clear that simplifying slogans like "the feminization of poverty" (which implies that gender is the only determinant of poverty) are effective. For Black women who experience discrimination because of both race and gender, the "feminization of poverty" may be an alienating way of referring to problems that are only partly, and probably not primarily, gender-based.

Defining the Interests of Black Women

Black women's special status has been frequently ignored both by researchers and by activists whose goal seems to be to project an image of a unified, homogeneous "women's movement." Their assumption that all women have similar or even identical interests has roots in the political need to represent more women, and, understandably, to advance the position of women as a distinct social group.

It is appropriate, indeed, to question the strength of women's "coalitions" and to test the gossamer threads that frequently hold such coalitions together. Although the left or progressives may have identified a common agenda, the importance of certain items may still be a matter for some disagreement. It is tempting to confuse goals of political moderates with those of the political left, but the symbolism of "women's equality" in political arenas may have little meaning for Black communities and for Black women in particular.

This is particularly important when we note that the way we have measured gains and improvements in both the status of Blacks and the status of women has been by pointing to the attainment of power or employment in political, corporate, and other elite arenas. But even as these measurable gains (for example, in the number of women elected officials) are achieved, it is appropriate to question their underlying significance. Are powerful women feminists? Are they concerned with the advancement of women? Are they progressives, concerned with a more just society? Do they share our vision of economic power: decent work at decent pay? Lyndon Johnson's almost all-white Women's Commission decided in the mid-sixties that women's greatest problem was their lack of household help. The federal government then spent millions of dollars training women, mostly those of color, to be maids. Empowerment is simultaneously a political and an economic process. While we may be pleased as women move into influential jobs, we may wonder if these women can share the benefits of their position with the still vast majority of women who occupy the lower strata of the nation's economy.

If women were to write the rules to help women attain economic power, what kind of rules might they write? Possibly, rules to implement comparable worth, or equal pay for jobs of equal value. We might do this because we understand that comparable worth bridges the intentional gap between the Equal Pay Law and the Civil Rights Act. But would women write rules to help overcome the limitations of comparable worth? Comparable worth helps employed women, not the unemployed, who are disproportionately women of color. Would women write rules to ensure full employment? Would women write rules to protect women from the "contracting out" process which restricts women in service occupations, especially women of color, to low-paying jobs?

If women were to write the rules, they would only be able to write them because they walk into the political arena in significant numbers. When women sit down at the bargaining table, they have access to power by virtue of being able to say: "I represent several thousand women." But to mobilize those numbers and wield real power, some women have played games with others. Some have become "women pimps," or "feminization of poverty pimps." Are women together in their quest for power? A careful review of the politics that have surrounded the "feminization of poverty" suggests a rather different assessment.

The 1984 presidential and vice-presidential nomination process illustrated some of the differences between Black and white women and some of the limitations in political symbolism. While women's organizations like NOW and the National Women's Political Caucus pressured Walter Mondale to put a woman on the ticket, the women of Jesse Jackson's Rainbow Coalition worked for the passage of four minority planks in the Democratic platform. The Jackson positions included a reduction in the defense budget, a position repudiating first use of nuclear weapons, a commitment to affirmative action, and the elimination of run-off primaries. Although the Rainbow Coalition and groups of white women had hoped to cooperate at the convention on the passage of the minority planks, these efforts collapsed when Mondale announced, several days before the convention opened, that Geraldine Ferraro was his choice for a running mate. In an open letter to the National Women's Political Caucus, women of the Rainbow expressed their outrage that minority women's interests had been ignored. White women's organizations, unsurprisingly, celebrated the placing of a woman on the ticket. Women of color could reasonably demand: did Geraldine Ferraro's candidacy make it more likely that the hungry would be fed? That the homeless would be housed? That institutional racism would come to a screeching halt? That nuclear weapons were less likely to be used? That defense spending would be cut? That the budget would balance? Those women of the Rainbow Coalition who circulated the open letter thought not, and they justifiably resented Ferraro's candidacy (and Mondale's selection process, which blatantly ignored them and those whom they represented).

The broad claims that feminization of poverty theorists have made concerning women's poverty are grossly inadequate where women of color are concerned. The political coalitions some white women hope to build will be weak and narrow, not strong and empowering, because these women cannot sit down at the negotiating table and say "I represent women," since they manifestly do not speak for women of color.

What some women may see as important are issues other women see as low priorities. The 1984 Women's Economic Equity Act and its impact illustrate this point. The act had five provisions, proposing: reform in tax and retirement matters; dependent care; insurance payments; regulatory reform; and child-support enforcement. Of the five, the provisions to provide dependent care are of most interest to a broad cross-section of women. Childcare legislation is important to women of color and to poor women because it would make the dependent care credit refundable, thus aiding those women whose incomes are too low to make use of tax credits. The legislation is also important because it would provide communities with funds to make childcare referral information available. But the childcare provisions of the Economic Equity Act did not pass.

Women of color and poor women recognize little of interest in the other four provisions of the Economic Equity Act. The tax and retirement reforms would affect few Black women, since so many of them head families, and since so many of their spouses do not participate in the primary labor market where high taxes and pension benefits prevail. The treatment of pensions as a property right, while important for some women, may mean little to many minority women.

Provisions to enforce child-support judgments were also part of the Economic Equity Act. Because the earnings of many Black men are so low, Black women will gain little from "mandatory wage assignment" for child-support benefits. Where Black men earn marginal wages, the mandatory reduction of wages to pay child support may make it less advantageous for these men to participate in the legal labor-force. While no one would argue that Black men should be exempt from paying child support, high poverty rates in the Black community suggest that job creation would save more Black children from poverty than will mandatory enforcement of child-support awards.

The provisions of the Economic Equity Act that would reform insurance policies and gender bias in regulations seem to have a race-neutral effect on women. However, because more Black women earn low wages than do white women, fewer Black women have access to insurance, medical, and other wage insurance policies. Thus, these items may have a higher priority in a "women's agenda" than in a "Black women's agenda." Why should women of color use their political capital to support a legislative package that has nothing in it for them? Why help white middle-class women gain insurance rights, when these women have not helped women of color gain childcare benefits?

This discussion suggests that the issue of class is important in determining how women define power, and how Black and white women differ in the policy arena. Some women see economic power as securing raises and promotions. But one woman's raise might represent another woman's salary. Women who hire household help sometimes perpetuate women's lack of economic power by hiring female employees at less than decent wages.

While symbolism may differ for Black and white women, there does exist a set of issues important for all women. Childcare is a critical issue to working mothers regardless of race, income or occupation. As the number of women in the labor-force has risen, affordable childcare has not grown proportionately. Despite the potential unity among women that could be developed by working on this issue, no national organization has emerged to place childcare availability at the top of the "women's agenda." Instead, many national women's groups have focused on comparable worth, an issue clearly important for both Black and white women, especially those employed in government. The problem with using comparable worth as a unifying issue, however, is that many Black women are not measurably helped by comparable worth. Unskilled and semi-skilled workers, unemployed workers, and those whose jobs are contracted out gain very little from this sort of pay equalization.

Still it may be possible for a broadly based political movement to address the needs of all women, especially of women in poverty. But such a movement would need to frankly acknowledge the conflicts between the gender interests and the class interests of women. Moreover, as it developed a legislative agenda it would need to highlight those programs, like childcare (rather than pension reform), which have maximum benefit for *all* women, regardless of race and class.

Those who write about the "feminization of poverty" note that "two out of three adults in poverty are women." And they ask: "What if we were all to go to the polls?" Black women represent more than a third of these female adults in poverty. If they reject white women's leadership in a political movement that has the economic status of women at its foundation, and if they choose not to join white women at the polls, then a "woman's coalition" based on economic status will be narrow in scope and politically weak. This is especially true if white women's commitment to a "poor women's" agenda is as temporary as their conditions of poverty may be. Without the support of Black women, a political movement around women's issues will necessarily remain limited and fragile, destined ultimately to fail.

A discussion of women, power and politics is, of necessity, a discussion that raises more questions than it answers. But by exposing the underlying contradictions in the slogan "feminization of poverty" it becomes clear that the political economy of Black women as a distinct group is indispensable to the development of a "women's agenda." No political movement can be galvanized around gender until the differential status of women of color is recognized in the programs of the women's movement. Both Black and white women are demonstrably disadvantaged in the economic structures of the contemporary United States, but the weight of poverty falls more heavily and for different reasons upon the former than the latter. Acknowledging this fact is the first preliminary step to forging a truly powerful coalition of all women who suffer the effects of an inhuman capitalist marketplace. To the "politics of gender," we must perforce add a politics of race and class.

Notes

1. Marianne Ferber, "Women and Work: Issues of the 1980s," *Signs* 8, 2 (Winter 1982), pp. 273–95.

2. Gloria Hull, Patricia Bell Scott and Barbara Smith, eds, *But Some of Us Are Brave: Black Women's Studies* (Old Westbury, NY: Feminist Press, 1982).

3. *Corporations and Two Career Families*, New York: Catalyst Career and Family Centre, 1980.

4. Ann Harlan and Carol L. Weiss, "Sex Differences in Factors Affecting Managerial Career Advancement," in Phyllis A. Wallace, ed., *Women in the Workplace: Management of Human Resources* (Boston, Ma.: Auburn House, 1982).

5. Shirley Harkess, 'Women's Occupational Experiences in the 1970s: Sociology and Economics," *Signs* 10, 3 (Spring 1985).

6. Cynthia Fuchs Epstein, *Women in Law* (New York: Basic Books, 1981).

7. Cynthia Fuchs Epstein, "Positive Effects of the Multiple Negative: Explaining the Success of Black Professional Women," *American Journal of Sociology* 78, 4 (January 1973).

8. Kathryn M. Langwell, "Factors Affecting the Incomes of Men and Women Physi-

cians: Further Explorations," *Journal of Human Resources* 14, 2 (Spring 1982), pp. 261–75.

9. Dennis N. DeTray and David H. Greenberg, "On Estimating Sex Differences in Earnings," *Southern Economic Journal* 44 (October 1977), pp. 348–53.

10. Charles R. Link and Russell F. Settle, "Labor Supply Responses of Married Professional Nurses: New Evidence," *Journal of Human Resources* 14, 2 (Spring 1979), pp. 235–76.

11. US Department of Commerce, "Money Income and Poverty Status of Families and Persons in the United States: 1982," Series P-60, no. 140 (1983).

12 Diana Pearce, "The Feminization of Poverty: Women, Work and Welfare," *Urban and Social Change Review* (February 1978).

13. Wendy Sarvesy, "Fighting the Feminization of Poverty: Socialist Feminist Analysis and Strategy," Presented at the Union of Radical Political Economists Meeting (1983).

14. Women's Economic Agenda Project, "Women's Economic Agenda: A Call to Action By and For California Women" (Oakland, California, 1984).

15. Julianne Malveaux, "Similarities and Differences in the Economic Interests of Black and White Women," *Review of Black Political Economy* (Summer 1985).

16. Pamela Sparr, "Re-evaluating Feminist Economics," *Dollars and Sense* No. 99 (September 1984).

17. Richard Freeman, *Black Elite* (New York: Mc Graw Hill, 1976); James P. Smith and Finis Welch, "Race Differences in Earnings: A Survey and New Evidence" (Santa Monica, Calif.: The Rand Corporation, March 1978).

18. William Darity, "Illusions of Black Progress," *Review of Black Political Economy* 10 (Winter 1980), pp. 153–68.

19. Steven Shulman, "The Measurement and Interpretation of Black Wage and Occupational Gains: A Reevaluation," *Review of Black Political Economy* 12, 4 (Spring 1984).

20. Timothy Bates, "Black Economic Well-Being Since the 1960s," *Review of Black Political Economy* 12, 4 (Spring 1984).

21. Julianne Malveaux, "Shifts in the Occupational and Employment Status of Black Women: Current Trends and Future Implications," *Black Working Women: Debunking the Myths, A Multidisciplinary Approach* (Berkeley, Calif.: UC Berkeley Women's Center, 1981).

22. Julianne Malveaux, "Theoretical Explanations of the Persistence of Racial Unemployment Differentials," in William Darity, ed., *Labor Economics: Modern Views* (Boston, 1984).

23. Phyllis Wallace, *Black Women in the Labor Force* (Cambridge, Ma: MIT Press, 1980).

24. Bates, "Black Economic Well-Being."

25. Ibid.

26. Barbara Jones, "Black Women and Labor Force Participation: An Analysis of Sluggish Growth Rates," *Review of Black Political Economy* vol. 14, No. 3 (Winter 1986).

27. Julianne Malveaux, "Low Wages Black Women: Occupational Descriptions, Strategies for Change," NAACP Legal Defense and Education Fund, 1984.

28. Julianne Malveaux, "Black Women's Employment in Recession and Recovery," American Educators Association meetings, December 1985.

29. Ibid.

30. Julianne Malveaux, "Recent Trends in Occupational Segregation by Race and Sex," Paper presented May 1982 to the Committee on Women's Employment and Related Social Issues, National Academy of Sciences.

31. Malveaux, "Low Wages Black Women."

32. Ibid.

33. Bureau of Labor Statistics, "BLS Reports on Displaced Workers," November 1984.

34. Malveaux, "Theoretical Explanations."

35. Bureau of Labor Statistics, "The Employment Situation: September 1984."

3

The Black Underclass as Systemic Phenomenon

Mack Jones

The notion that the United States is now characterized by an emerging permanent Black underclass has been commonplace in both the scholarly and popular literature since the mid 1970s.[1] The "discovery" of the Black underclass has been accompanied by predictions of the dire social consequences which may follow if ameliorative action is not undertaken. As of now, however, no significant national programs have been developed to address the problems of the Black underclass. This is so, at least in my opinion, because the presence of the Black underclass is a logical, perhaps even necessary, outgrowth of the American political economy conditioned by white racism. That is to say, the presence of the Black underclass is not a result of either malfunctioning of the American economic process or of the pathology of the members of the underclass. The underclass results from the sum of the routine systemically prescribed actions of the constituent elements or institutions of the political economy. If that is the case, and at least one man is convinced that it is, then nothing short of fundamental changes in the politico-economic system can solve the problem of the Black underclass.

One of the purposes of this essay, then, is to offer an explanation of the presence of the Black underclass as a systemic phenomenon. A second objective is to assess the implications of the presence of the Black underclass for the future of the struggle for racial equality in the United States.

We may begin by clarifying who or what is the Black underclass and how it came into being, before moving on to discuss how various constituent institutions of the political economy create and maintain the conditions which give rise to the Black underclass. What is the Black underclass? In both the popular and scholarly literature the concept remains a bit fuzzy and imprecise. It is generally understood to refer to a growing number of Black persons who are uneducated, unskilled, unemployed and often unemployable, or employed in low-paying jobs, living in unrelieved poverty, and immersed in a culture conditioned by such abject circumstances, with only limited chances or hope for upward mobility.

Harsh as the foregoing recitation of conditions may sound, they are in no way novel conditions or new developments among Black Americans. These conditions have dogged the Black nation throughout American history. If these conditions have always characterized a sizeable proportion of the Black population how do we explain the use of the term "emerging Black underclass," implying, as it were, that it is a new phenomenon. The key to understanding this conceptualization is the use of the adjective "permanent." The term is used to imply that members of the present underclass differ from earlier editions by the fact that the former and their progeny are destined to remain in circumstances which characterize the underclass while members of the earlier underclass were more upwardly mobile. Simply put, the argument seems to be that the present underclass is intergenerational and self-perpetuating while its antecedents were more transient.

This perception of the permanent underclass is misleading, in my view, both historically and conceptually, and it leads to misguided and inappropriate public policies. It is misleading historically because it assumes that the underclass is a new development without providing any evidence, either scientific or anecdotal, to support the claim. It is conceptually flawed because by its narrow focus on the characteristics of the members of the underclass it obscures the symmetrical relationship between the rise of the conditions which entrap the underclass and the routine operations of basic societal forces.

Rather than conceptualizing the current Black underclass as a new development, it may be more historically accurate and theoretically insightful to view it as a contemporary manifestation of a long-existing phenomenon. I suggest this because if the defining characteristic of the underclass is the absence of realistic chances for upward mobility, there has always been a sizeable segment of the Black population destined to such a fate.

The current edition of the underclass is the residual of a much larger impoverished group of Black poor which existed prior to the unprecedented spiral of Black upward mobility experienced during the 1960s. Within this larger historically constant collection of Black poor, there was always a core of persons for whom there was no realistic chance of being integrated into the socio-economic system as productive self-sustaining actors. If such was the case historically as one pattern of production and the accompanying socio-economic and culture systems gave way to the next, it would mean that the presence of the underclass is not to be explained by the particularities of a given historical constant. These would be systemic forces rather than individual or group pathologies.

I shall return to this point later, but first I wish to review and comment on some of the key assumptions about the size, location and nature of the underclass. This review and commentary will demonstrate that the gap between black and white economic well-being on almost all indicators has been and continues to be constant and symmetrical and therefore systemic. That is to say, the conditions of Blacks and whites fluctuate in tandem in response to changes in the economy. I will also argue that the constantly high level of Black poverty and its three to one ratio to white poverty are simply two indicators of the systemic character of black deprivation and that underclass status is simply the lowest point on that continuum of black deprivation.

Most commentators, both scholarly and popular, identify the Black underclass as an urban phenomenon and a product of the pathos of the inner city. Typically, studies begin by identifying census tracts with large concentrations of low-income people and labeling them as underclass neighborhoods. Using this method, Sawhill speculated that less than 6 per cent of the Black population live in underclass neighborhoods.[2]

While the literature tells us that underclass persons are to be found in certain neighborhoods and that members of the underclass are likely to have certain accompanying characteristics, it offers no criteria for determining which individuals are in fact part of the underclass. No one claims that all residents of such neighborhoods are members of the underclass. Nor does anyone claim that all of those who share certain accompanying characteristics such as teenage motherhood are members of the underclass. Some use the idea of "dysfunctional underclass behaviors" to distinguish between the routine (non-system threatening) poor and the underclass. However, this distinction turns out to be more illusory than real because the presence of these behaviors is inferred from aggregate statistics. Thus, we have no empirically useful definition of the underclass; at least not one which would allow us to predict which individuals are members of it.[3]

Finally, as mentioned earlier, the literature conveys the impression that the underclass is a new or emerging and growing problem. This argument is supported primarily by the finding that the number of poor

Blacks living in poverty-stricken neighborhoods has increased. However, while the residential concentration of the Black poor has grown, the proportion of both individuals and families living in poverty has actually decreased over the last three decades. In fact, it is the escape of middle-income and upwardly mobile Black poor which isolates and makes the residual underclass more visible.

Between 1959 and 1969, for example, the proportion of Black individuals living in poverty decreased sharply from 55 to 32 per cent;[4] the figure dropped to 30 per cent in 1971 before rising to 33 per cent in 1980 where it remained in 1987. The decline in poverty among Black families showed a similar pattern, falling from 48 per cent in 1959 to 27.9 per cent in 1969. Since that time it has vacillated between 27 per cent and the 1987 rate of 33 per cent. Thus, it appears that the upward mobility of Black individuals and families, as expressed through income, peaked around 1969 and that a Black poverty rate of 30–33 per cent, roughly three times the rate of whites, is the new norm.

The actual number of Black persons living in poverty, however, is only slightly less than the 1959 figure of 9.9 million. The number dropped to its lowest level of 7.1 million in 1969. It returned to 9.9 million in 1983 and dropped to 9 million in 1986.

The systemic character of Black poverty is also reflected in its regional and spatial distribution. Historically, for well-known reasons, the poverty rate among Southern Blacks exceeded that of Blacks living elsewhere. However, following the dissolution of the racial caste system in the 1970s, conditions in the South began to approximate those in other regions. By 1987, the South had a poverty rate of 34.5 per cent, down from the 41 per cent which obtained in 1969. In the Midwest in 1987, 36.6 per cent of Blacks were classified as poor while 28.8 per cent in the West were poor.[5]

Regarding place of residence, in 1987 the poverty rate among Black families remained highest in non-metropolitan areas – 40 per cent as compared to 27.8 per cent in metropolitan areas. Within metropolitan areas, the Black poverty rate was 30.7 per cent inside and 21.1 per cent outside central cities. The Black to white ratio was 3.8 for metropolitan and 3.6 for non-metropolitan areas. Black poverty among persons classified as rural farm was 30 per cent in 1980.

What picture can be drawn from the poverty data presented in the preceding paragraphs and what implications are there for our efforts to understand the nature and predicament of the Black underclass? Perhaps most significantly, the data show that Black poverty is not a localized or particularized phenomenon. It ranges from 30–35 per cent throughout every region of the country except for the West. It is higher among non-metropolitan than metropolitan Blacks and the poverty rate among rural farm Blacks is greater than the rate among Blacks living in the central city.

The data also show that the Black poverty rate dropped significantly between 1959 and 1969, but has not changed measurably since that time. As a matter of fact, since 1970 the proportion of Black individuals living in poverty has increased in every region of the country except the South. Only the South, the most laggard region in 1970, showed a significant decrease, from 42.6 to 34.5 per cent in 1987. Also, the Black to white poverty ratio for the country has remained almost unchanged – it was 3.3 in 1969 and 3.1 in 1987, although it went as high as 3.7 in 1972 and 1973.

When figures on Black unemployment rates, family income, and labor-force participation rates and Black to white ratios on these indicators are added to the picture, they lend additional credence to the claim that Black economic fortunes are systemic. The Black unemployment rate is constantly approximately double the white rate while the median income of Black families is almost always at least one-third less than that for whites.

Regarding labor-force participation, during the period immediately following emancipation and continuing into the early decades of the twentieth century, the labor-intensive economy needed large numbers of menial workers. During this period when higher participation rates were more of an indicator of relative deprivation than economic well-being, both Black men and women had higher participation rates. However, as the socio-economic system changed and high labor-force participation rates became essential for family and community well-being, Black access to the labor-force was constricted. Black men were pushed out of the labor-force and the rate of increase for Black women was considerably less than that of white women. For example, in 1930, 80 per cent of Black males and almost 40 per cent of Black females were in the labor-force compared to only 76 per cent and 20 per cent of white men and women, respectively. By 1989, the rate for Black men had fallen to 69 per cent and that for Black women was up to 58 per cent. The 1985 rates for white men and women were 76 and 57 per cent, respectively.

This shows that the economic fortunes of Blacks in comparison to those of whites ebb and flow in a non-random fashion. Black well-being on practically all indicators remains only a predictable fraction of white well-being regardless of historical, geographical or economic circumstances. The logical conclusion is that they are all driven by some larger force.

Assuming that the Black underclass is an unspecified proportion of the Black poor, the data discussed above question the popular notion that the underclass is essentially an urban phenomenon sustained by the resumed anomic culture or residential isolation of inner-city Blacks. The poverty rate is actually higher among non-metropolitan Blacks and the "objective" conditions associated with the underclass – that is, welfare dependency, high unemployment and unemployability, high incidence of criminal activity, etc. – are as common in the small and medium size towns and rural areas of the South as they are in the megalopoles of the North.

Again, this suggests that one key to understanding the problem of the Black underclass is to view it as a systemic development. That is to say that when the US political economy is operating routinely, it routinely creates the conditions which give rise to the underclass. To pursue this argument let me return to my earlier conceptualization of the permanent underclass as a residual category.

Following the end of slavery and continuing until 1959, the preponderant majority of the Black population was classified as poor. However, as the then labor-intensive economy grew and underwent various structural changes, so did the demand for labor, including Black labor. This created windows of opportunity and fueled an extended period of upward mobility for the Black population. Consequently, the most salient characteristic of the Black poor, until the current historical moment, was upward mobility. This fitted nicely with and reinforced the prevailing myth that those who remain in poverty have only themselves to blame.

However, there have always been those among the poor who have no realistic chance for upward mobility. They are simply submerged among the larger number of upwardly mobile poor. In earlier periods, the underclass obviously constituted a smaller proportion of the poor population, but as more and more of the upwardly mobile poor were absorbed into non-poverty positions, the underclass became more pronounced among the poor; they were the residuals.

Rather than beginning with the tautological assumption that the conditions under which the underclass live explain their condition, a more promising approach might be to try to establish the extent to which the conditions of the underclass are generated by societally sanctioned institutions and practices of the US political economy. I suggest this because it is widely acknowledged that cultures evolve as a result of the efforts of a people to adapt to the environment in which they exist. Thus the so-called culture of poverty or the Wilsonian cultural isolation can be viewed as the response to certain conditions rather than the reverse.[6] This is not to deny the obvious, that is, that certain behavioral problems make members of the underclass less attractive to potential employers, rather it is to sharpen the focus by raising the question of what factors account for the rise of widespread poverty disproportionately among blacks. The answer, I would argue, is to be found in the undeniable laws of American capitalism as conditioned by white supremacy as a dominant American value.

Income inequality and income immobility have always been two major laws of American capitalist development. For example, the poorest 10 per cent of the population received 3.4 per cent of the national income in 1910 and 1.1 per cent in 1959, while the figures for the wealthiest tenth were 33.9 in 1910 and 28.9 in 1959. Income differentials ranging from excessive opulence to grinding poverty are expected and legitimized by the prevailing American ideology. Poverty is considered not an anomaly but an expected outcome of the economy.

So too is unemployment. Full employment has been defined as 4 to 6 per cent unemployment and it has been established for some time now that even such levels of employment are rarely attained during peacetime. And Black unemployment is always around twice the white rate. The American political economy routinely creates a sizeable number of persons without incomes sufficient to meet their most basic needs. Since production of goods and services in the US political economy responds to effective demand as opposed to need, persons with limited incomes are unable to command access to a reasonable share of available goods and services through socially sanctioned procedures. As a consequence, a whole array of debilities – poor health care, poor housing, and poor education – befall them. Seen in this way, these debilities are routine outgrowths of the US economic process. The fact that they have remained constants in American life in spite of the impressive advantages which have been made in science and technology illustrates this point.

Under these circumstances we are justified in assuming that the economy gives rise to the debilities, and that institutional practices governed by the principle of white supremacy result in the disproportionate allocation of these debilities among Black Americans. As discussed earlier, Black poverty remained approximately three times that of whites over the last quarter century and Black unemployment is almost always twice that of whites. Comparable differentials exist between Blacks and whites on practically every measure of socioeconomic well-being and these differentials exist among all categories of Blacks and whites. The white wealthy are wealthier and the Black poor are poorer.

Race becomes the criterion for allocating to Black Americans a disproportionate share of the debilities which are routinely created by the economy. This argument may be controversial but I believe that there is sufficient anecdotal evidence available to justify giving it serious attention and rigorous empirical testing. Let me proceed to make the anecdotal case.

Most observers cite poor education, poor health care and inferior work experience as major constituents of the problem of the underclass. My thesis that the presence of the Black underclass is a systemic function would be given credence if it can be demonstrated that the abovementioned problems are created and sustained by the routine activities of legitimate economic and political institutions and actors. For purposes of illustration, let us analyze the problems of education.

Poor education and the lack of skills and satisfactory work experience derived therefrom are often cited as *the* major problem of the permanent underclass. To what extent, we may ask, do the structure and function of the American educational system help create and sustain the problems of the underclass? Presently and historically, post-secondary educational training has been the major avenue for Black upward mobility. However, the post-secondary educational system in the United States is organized and funded in a manner which benefits the more privileged elements at the expense of the poor and current trends exacerbate rather than relieve the problems of the underclass. This is so, at least partially, because post-secondary educational systems are arranged and funded in a hierarchical fashion which reinforces the current unequal distribution of both competencies and income.

As Alexander Astin has pointed out, in the US public post-secondary educational systems are organized in a hierarchical fashion with universities being at the apex, followed by high selective four-year colleges, medium selective, low selective four-year colleges and then two-year colleges.[7] Admission standards and other practices result in a class stratified scholastic population with high-status persons attending the universities and lower-status students in the two-year institutions.

The funding of public post-secondary education reinforces the class hierarchy. The more selective the institutions the greater the per student subsidiary provided by the state. Astin's 1975 data is presented in Table 5. As one goes up the hierarchical education ladder, the number of Black students diminishes proportionately.[8] In 1976, 42 per cent of all Black students enrolled in higher education were in two-year colleges and only 15 per cent were enrolled at the university level.[9]

A rational interplanetary visitor might expect to find a direct correla-

Table 5　Dollars Per FTE Student

Type of Institution	"Subsidy" educational & general plus aid expenditures minus tuition ($)
Two-year colleges	1,208
Four-year colleges	
Low Selectivity	1,253
Medium Selectivity	1,448
High Selectivity	2,179
Universities	
Low Selectivity	2,744
Medium Selectivity	2,850
High Selectivity	5,205

tion between the size of the educational subsidy per student and the presumed educational difficulties of the student body, that is, the greater the educational problems and financial needs of the student, the greater the subsidy. However, as these data show, just the opposite is the case. As Astin asserts,

Thus the subsidy is smallest in those institutions enrolling the poorest students, and greatest in those institutions enrolling the most well to do . . . Here again is another important side-effect of a hierarchically arranged public system based upon selective admission: students who are denied access to the universities and more selective four-year colleges (including a disproportionate share of the low income and minority students) receive substantially less public subsidy for their post-secondary education than do students who manage to enter the more selective public colleges and universities.[10]

Clearly, the post-secondary educational system reinforces the existing class differences and hardly anyone would dispute the assertion that elementary and secondary school systems operate in a similar manner and have a similar effect. Indeed the current move toward competency tests as prerequisites for a high school diploma will only aggravate the problem. Competency tests superimposed upon the existing educational system only insure that even larger numbers of poor children will not receive high school diplomas and, inasmuch as the diplomas are an arbitrary prerequisite for many entry-level jobs, chances for upward mobility are limited even more.

The winnowing process of the educational system dovetails with the imperatives of the job market. Inasmuch as the economy does not provide sufficient well-paying jobs for the total population, a significant proportion of workers must be content with jobs paying poverty-level wages while still others can only find intermittent work. "Objective" criteria can be used to ration the limited hierarchically arranged work opportunities. The educational system insures that these "objective" capabilities are distributed among the population in a predictable non-random class and racially biased fashion.

Just as the education system reinforces the conditions which give rise to and sustains the circumstances within which the underclass is trapped, so do the housing and finance systems. Wilson has argued that the isolation of the underclass in inner-city crime-infested neighborhoods is a primary cause of its permanency. To the extent that this is the case, it seems obvious that this isolation is the result of the community sanctioned behavior of such diverse actors as bankers, real estate brokers, owners of industrial capital and retail outlets, as well as the more prosperous gainfully employed workers.

It is eminently sensible for the owners of industrial capital and the growing service industries to follow their preferred predominantly white labor-force to the suburbs. And it is just as sensible for the conglomerate-owned retail and service outlets to follow suit. Similarly, bankers are not being illogical in a capitalist system grounded in white supremacy when they choose to finance white-dominated suburban rather than central city developments. Mayors and city councils, in turn, are doing what they are expected to do when they support tax schemes, transportation systems, and labor-force growth policies which favor the already privileged at the expense of the poor in order to "revitalize" the inner city. And, finally, middle-income Blacks who have the wherewithal to escape the decadence of the central city are also behaving quite rationally when they follow their white compatriots to the suburbs. The outcome, of course, of this confluence of self-interested and community-sanctioned behaviors is the perpetuation of the conditions which entrap the underclass – a deteriorating housing stock, substandard schools, limited job opportunities, welfare dependency, crime and unrelieved poverty. If these conditions which entrap the underclass are systemic, the phenomenon itself must be systemically based as well.

Let me conclude this essay with a brief comment on the implications of the conditions which entrap the Black underclass for the future of the struggle for racial equality in the United States. As a residual phenomenon, the permanent Black underclass is at once a monument to the successful protest activity of the civil rights movement and a reminder of its theoretical barrenness. The activists and theoreticians of the movement never articulated a full-blown political philosophy which would have allowed them to understand and explain the connection between the economic and political dimensions of the unequal conditions of Black Americans. There was, however, an unarticulated but widely shared assumption among them that the end of state-sanctioned segregation and discrimination would set in motion a train of events which would lead to economic parity between whites and Black Americans. And it was assumed, at least implicitly, that Black economic parity could be achieved without significant material cost to whites and without fundamental changes in the economic system.

The theoretical barrenness of this position became obvious when the combination of slackened economic growth, certain structural changes in the economy, and the accelerated entrance of women into the labor-force precipitated circumstances which produced a white counter-movement.

The decline of the industrial sector, especially in the Midwest, eliminated many of the well-paying jobs that provided a comfortable living and upward mobility for working-class Black families. At the same time, the newly created service-sector jobs paid less than those in the industrial sector and called for skills not found among the majority of the displaced industrial workers. Moreover, inasmuch as more and more women were entering the labor-force, the displaced industrial workers had to compete with more and often better qualified workers for the newly created and lower-paying service-sector jobs.

During this period of economic dislocation and structural change, whites interpreted Black demands as a call for white loss of status, reverse racism, as it were. Generally, whites argued that racism and racial discrimination were no longer societal problems and that any remaining differences between the races were functions of objective differences in individual qualifications and hence not amenable to group remedies. Qualifications and competency tests became shibboleths of the white counter-movement. Access to educational institutions, attractive job opportunities and on-the-job promotions would be determined by "objective" criteria as reflected in test scores.

Predictably, these criteria could be satisfied by only a disproportionately small segment of Black aspirants. And this segment has made impressive economic progress. The result, however, has been intensification of income inequality within the Black community. Thus, as the small number of "qualified" Blacks prospered many more slipped into poverty and into the underclass.

The implications of this development for the future of the struggle for racial equality depend to a great extent on the interpretation given to it by Black political and intellectual leadership. That leadership in all probability will continue to come from that segment of the community which benefited most from the gains of the civil rights era. They and their progeny will be more able to meet the imposed competency tests and as a result, they will continue to prosper economically. As they continue to prosper, they may justifiably claim that their good fortune is the result of their own hard work. They may argue that they played the meritocracy game and won.

Meanwhile, the underclass will become relatively more impoverished and increasingly wards of the state. Middle-class Black professionals will staff the societal institutions which administer to, and manage the lives of, the underclass. And, as middle-class Blacks inherit governmental power in more and more of the country's major cities, Blacks will man those public outposts responsible for protecting the dominant propertied classes from the rebellious reactions of the underclass.

To date, most of the Black political leadership has refused to join mainstream white interests who blame the underclass for their own unhappy state. They have insisted that the causes are to be found in more fundamental economic forces conditioned by institutional racism. However, they have shied away from exploring the systemic nature of the underclass phenomenon and as a result, they have no program or plan of action for addressing the problem.

Perhaps surprisingly, Black intellectual leadership has been much more inclined to accept the argument that the plight of the underclass is of their own making. A group of strategically placed Black intellectuals in prestigious Eastern universities have played a leading role in propagating this thesis. Through their works, which are published in influential policy-oriented journals and magazines, they reinforce the conventional claim that the problems of the underclass are primarily problems internal to the Black community and evidence of the failure of Black leadership, and the selfishness of the Black middle class from which that leadership arises. And in turn, these intellectuals help create a climate which allows a hostile or indifferent white leadership to create, cultivate and elevate to prominence a new reactionary Black leadership class. The new Black leadership class, as demonstrated by certain Black leaders who achieved prominence during the Reagan era, is prepared to join forces with the most conservative forces in society on matters involving race and public policy. Whether white conservatives are successful in creating a new Black leadership class will be a key element in determining how Black leadership interprets the problem of the underclass.

If Black leadership views the underclass as a systemic problem, it may force a public debate on the dialectical relationship between poverty and wealth, between affluence and decadence and between privilege and deprivation. Such a point of departure would at least stimulate a national debate on the systemic character of the problem of the underclass. And it could be the first shot in a real war against poverty.

Notes

1. Among scholarly writings one of the more sytematic if not more enlightened interpretations of the emergence of the Black underclass can be found in William J. Wilson, *The Declining Significance of Race* (Chicago: University of Chicago Press, 1978). For an enlightened case study of underclass youth in Los Angeles see Douglas Glasgow, *The Black Underclass* (New York: Vintage Books, 1981).

2. Isabel Sawhill "An Overview," *Public Interest* no. 96 (Summer 1989), p. 6.

3. Doubt about this term has been expressed even by those most associated with it; see Thomas B. Edsall, "Underclass Term Falls From Favor," *Washington Post*, August 13, 1990.

4. Barbara A. Jones, "Patterns and Trends of Black Poverty and Welfare Recipiency," Working Paper Series, Southern Center for Studies in Public Policies, Fall 1984 (Atlanta, Ga.).

5. Ibid.

6. William J. Wilson, *The Truly Disadvantaged* (Chicago: University of Chicago Press, 1987).

7. Alexander Astin, *The Myth of Equal Access in Public Higher Education* (Atlanta, Ga.: Southern Education Foundation, 1975).

8. Ibid., p. 12.

9. Bernard Watson, "The Quality of Education for Black Americans," *The State of Black America* (Baltimore, Md.: National Urban League, Inc., 1981), p. 76.

10. Astin, *The Myth*, pp. 12–13.

4

Understanding the Underclass: The Role of Culture and Economic Progress

Charles P. Henry

According to Genesis, work is the punishment for sin and the fate of humankind. Only those without sin may rest idle, and since we are all children of Adam and Eve we all carry the burden of original sin. Throughout history our attitudes toward our own employment as well as the work of others have constantly shifted while never losing a sense of tension or moral ambiguity. We admire the lifestyle of the idle rich while condemning the laziness of the poor. Our own status as individuals is integrally tied to our work but we constantly seek ways to increase our leisure time.

Our own views on work make it difficult to distinguish between the "deserving," "worthy" or "truly" poor. Like such terms as aristocracy, elite and underclass, definitions are imprecise and subjective. History provides little clear guidance in drawing such distinctions. Greek city-states generally felt that civic honor was compromised by the existence of beggars and such beggars were treated very harshly. Blame for one's unemployment fell on the individual and not the polity. Medieval society, on the other hand, was based on the Christian belief that poverty was a holy state, accepting alms no disgrace, and charity both a proof of piety and a key to eternal salvation. However, given limited resources, it was believed necessary to establish some priorities and St Augustine suggested that charity should not be given to those who "neglected righteousness."[1]

However, by making this moral distinction between idle persons, one also makes it possible to label some poor persons who work as undeserving. It is far from impossible to find hardworking sinners. And as the simple economic relations of feudal rural society broke down, so did the views of the upper classes who had looked down on any kind of manual labor. By the early sixteenth century, when we see the establishment of municipal poor laws and welfare institutions like the Aumone Generale of Lyons, civil authorities have replaced clerical authorities in controlling relief efforts.

In their efforts to organize and centralize assistance, new attempts were made to separate "sturdy beggars" from the "deserving" poor. The medieval assumption that work was available for all who would labor led to vocational training for the unskilled and public works at "reasonable and moderate" wages for those who could not find employment on their own.[2] Even these early efforts at vocational training through the apprenticing of poor children often ran into stiff opposition from the guilds.

This medieval assumption that work is available at fair wages for all who are willing to work is at the heart of contemporary debates about the underclass. One side assumes that there are plenty of jobs available but members of the underclass lack the character to pursue them. The other side of the debate questions both the quantity and quality of jobs available. The former side "blames the victim" while the latter side "blames the system." Yet neither side questions the very concept of the underclass itself.

Today it makes little sense to refer to a single underclass as a homogeneous economic unit with similar attitudes and values. Yet much of today's scholarly writing on the underclass makes this assumption. And although there is no agreed upon definition of the underclass, most writers identify its core as central-city Blacks.[3] By using class terminology while referring to a specific Black subculture, social observers and policy-makers are able to make moral pronouncements on the worthiness of aid recipients while ignoring the larger economic issues of growing income inequality in a changing economic structure and the declining political power of unions. An analysis of the "underclass" that looks at both race and class variables reveals a complex picture that narrowly conceived programs like workfare – or forcing recipients of public assistance to work in order to discourage dependency on government dole – cannot even begin to address. Only a comprehensive, integrated policy approach that emphasizes both the quantity and quality of jobs can meet the standard of both moral justice and economic practicality.

If the concept of the underclass is meant to define a group of people caught in a permanent cycle of poverty, it has done little to clarify their position or suggest solutions. Poverty as a condition of being in want of something that is needed, desired, or generally recognized as having value is not static in nature. It comes in varying degrees ranging from starvation and death from exposure to inadequate medical care. It differs from country to country. In Africa, for example, two levels of poverty have existed for several centuries. One level involves very large numbers of Africans who have continuously struggled to preserve themselves and their dependents from physical want. Another level involves a smaller group of persons who have permanently or temporarily failed in that struggle and are now destitute. There is no sharp dividing line between these groups although some might be tempted to call the latter an underclass. In fact, John Iliffe argues it is the convergence of structural poverty (long-term) and conjunctural poverty (temporary poverty) that characterizes and complicates much of twentieth-century African society.[4]

In the United States, the poor might be briefly defined as those who lack jobs or an adequate income. Those scholars who study the underclass have failed to define consistently the relationship of poverty to underclass status. If all persistently poor individuals (that is, individuals poor for eight of the last ten years) who are not disabled or aged are defined as part of the underclass, then 23.5 per cent of the poor, or 7–8 million persons, belong to the underclass. If we limit our definition to all poor Blacks and Latinos living in the nation's largest cities, then less than 16 per cent of the poor population, or 5.2 million persons, fit the definition. If we further limit the underclass to those with a high incidence of joblessness, high school dropouts, welfare dependents and female-headed families, then only 5 per cent of the poor population, or 1.6 million Americans, are in the underclass. Using the latter criteria Isabel Sawhill and Erol Ricketts found that 40 per cent of underclass census tracts are *not* in areas of extreme poverty and that 72 per cent of the census tracts with high poverty rates are not underclass tracts by behavioral definition.[5]

While low income and deviant social behavior are highly correlated, they are not the same. In his *Unheavenly City*, Edward Banfield distinguished between the middle classes who were able to defer immediate gratification for long-term gain and the lower classes who were not. Given the standard behavior of corporate executives in the United States in looking for short-term profits at the expense of long-term development and the typical behavior of the middle-class credit card holder, Banfield's distinction begins to fade.[6] A number of scholars, including Oscar Lewis, Lee Rainwater, Herbert J. Gans, Herbert Gutman, Elliot Liebow and others, believe that most of the poor share the values and aspirations of the working and middle classes. The divergence between their aspirations and their behavior is a function of their poverty. While each author places a differing degree of emphasis on the effects of poverty in terms of pathology, most view the behavior of the poor as realistic responses to a particular situation. The type of response may vary according to the individual. However, alternative norms are often developed to explain failure and provide support among peers.

If poverty and deviant social behavior are not synonymous, then what value or set of values link the members of the underclass together? It is our contention that, like the culture-of-poverty theorists, those who tend to use the concept of the underclass exaggerate class differences into polar opposites. That is, members of the underclass are portrayed as violent or lazy or seeking immediate gratification while the rest of us do not share such characteristics. It is our view that it is impossible to quantify such differences. To conceptualize underclass behavior in terms of a single dimension ignores differences in group behavior that are more qualitative than quantitative.

Several authors have argued that the contemporary underclass is not qualitatively different from the urban minority poor who migrated North in the decade following World War II. What distinguishes the contemporary underclass is the inability to get marginal jobs due to structural changes in the economy.[7] Yet this view is too simple if we want to argue that at least part of the underclass share mainstream values, for it is manifestly clear that mainstream values have changed over the last two decades.

Ulf Hannerz, for example, has identified the major materials ghetto-specific models utilize in constructing alternatives as norms which are actually supported by mainstream culture. These include strong, overt concerns with sexual exploitation, toughness and ability to command respect, personal appearance – with an emphasis on male clothing fashions – liquor consumption, and verbal ability.[8] It is important to note that Hannerz does not identify all ghetto males as supporting these norms. He indicates that "swingers" and "street-corner men" are more attracted to such normative models than "mainstreamers." In addition, Hannerz states that "[no] ghetto-specific model for a male–female union has anything close to the normative validity which the mainstream model enjoys in the ghetto as well as outside it, and this makes it hard for couples to find a state of the union which is as morally satisfying to them."[9] As the mainstream model declines, however, it must have some impact on those that had once aspired to it.

Ghetto-specific roles also seem to characterize the work of Ken Auletta, who helped popularize the term underclass. Using the Manpower Demonstration Research Corporation's (MDRC) estimate of 9 million persons in the underclass, Auletta divides them into four distinct categories: (a) the passive poor, usually long-term welfare recipients; (b) the hostile street criminals who terrorize most cities, and who are often school dropouts and drug addicts; (c) the hustlers who earn their living in an underground economy but rarely commit violent crimes; and (d) the traumatized drunks, drifters, homeless shopping-bag ladies and released patients. Auletta found members of the under-class from two-parent homes as well as members who subscribe to middle-class values. After five years in a supported work and skills training project, MDRC found that for two of the four target groups – ex-addicts and mothers receiving AFDC payments – "the benefits exceed the costs"; for ex-offenders the results were "inconclusive" and for youths the costs outweighed the benefits.[10]

Auletta's categories of the underclass contain groupings with very divergent characteristics. In what sense are the passive poor on welfare similar to the very active hustlers who some have argued are among the brightest minds, the young capitalists of the inner city? What values do the homeless share with drug dealers who often exhibit lavish life-styles? In fact it is difficult to find a reason to link such divergent groups together. Much of the work on Black youth demonstrates their active adjustment to their situation rather than passive acceptance. Black youth, like youth in general, are most apt to be in search of their first job (18 per cent) or to leave jobs in search of better employment. This situation contrasts significantly with the views of observers like Charles Murray and Martin Feldstein.[11]

In his study of young inner-city Blacks in Watts, Douglas Glasgow contends that their behaviors are consciously propagated through special socialization rituals that help them prepare for inequality at a very early age. As they grow older, young Blacks use these modes of behavior to neutralize the personally destructive effects of institutiona-lized racism. According to Glasgow, this "survival culture" differs significantly from the "culture of poverty" concept in that it is a very active rather than passive adaptation to reaction and distraction. Glasgow recognizes that while such a culture is situationally effective it may be dysfunctional if opportunities for independent development do arise.[12]

Drawing on a large survey of inner-city Black youth, Harry Holzer found evidence of dysfunctional behavior. For example, young Blacks seek jobs and wages that are comparable to those of young whites but that are at higher levels than the jobs and wages the young Blacks ultimately obtain. While these relative high expectations do lead to somewhat higher levels of non-employment, young Blacks appear at least as likely as whites to take specific low-skilled jobs, although they seem to accept them only temporarily. Both Blacks and whites are reluctant to take certain menial or dead-end jobs.[13]

Richard Freeman and Harry Holzer suggest that aging is not likely to solve the problem of Black employment because non-employed youth spend little time in activities that will raise their employability. At the same time these youth are not particularly satisfied with their lives and have a desire to engage in activities that could improve their future.[14] Further evidence of this desire is found in the labor market behavior of Black youth who respond positively to improved job quality. In reporting the findings of their empirical study, Ronald Ferguson and Randall Filer state that "inner-city Black youths behave rationally and that they can, therefore, be induced to modify their behavior by appropriately designed and targeted incentives."[15] Again, Freeman and Holzer state that their National Bureau of Economic Research survey yielded strong evidence that the state of the local labor market was a major determinant of youth joblessness. In Boston, for example, a city with a relatively strong labor market, inner-city Blacks had an employment rate 10 per cent above that of otherwise comparable youth in Chicago and Philadelphia, which have weaker labor markets.[16]

Of course, it is not impossible to find the stereotypical passive welfare mother or the carefree urban father that forms the focus of Murray's world-view, but empirical data present a different picture. In a large study of the unemployed, Kay Lehman Schlozman and Sidney Verba compare the distress of Blacks and whites. They report that Blacks, regardless of employment status, express more dissatisfaction than their white counterparts and those who are out of work, regardless of race, express more dissatisfaction than their working counterparts. The greatest gap in satisfaction was reported between whites with jobs and Blacks without: 28 per cent of the employed whites, as opposed to an overwhelming 90 per cent of the jobless Blacks, express dissatisfaction with income. Fifteen per cent of the working whites, as compared to 57 per cent of the unemployed Blacks, indicate dissatisfaction with their lives in general.[17] While 75 per cent of Blacks believe whites have an unfair advantage in getting good jobs as compared to 20 per cent of whites who think Blacks have the advantage, this does not lead to complacency or fatalism. Schlozman and Verba make clear that both working and jobless Blacks are even *more likely* than whites to make efforts to cope on their own.[18]

Given the variety of underclass responses to unemployment, what accounts for their inability to climb out of poverty? For many conservatives and some liberals, Black family structure has been identified as the primary culprit. However, other liberals have been inclined to point to changes in the structure of the economy and the increasing concentration and isolation of members of the underclass. From liberal journals like *The New Republic* and *The Atlantic Monthly* to the conservative *The Public Interest*, writers of all ideological persuasions have placed the blame and responsibility for the status of the Black underclass on the culture of the "victims." Mickey Kaus, writing in the former, states that "it is simply stupid to pretend that the culture of poverty isn't largely a Black culture."[19] Kaus cites Nicholas Lemann's article in *The Atlantic Monthly* which contends that "[t]he negative power of the ghetto culture all but guarantees that any attempt to solve the problems of the underclass *in the ghettos* won't work – the culture is too strong now."[20] In *The Public Interest*, Martin Kilson traces the growth of the underclass to the tremendous expansion of female-headed households during the last two decades. These households, says Kilson, "display a seemingly endemic incapacity to foster social mobility comparable to husband–wife and male-headed families."[21]

Popular media have joined the issue through such articles as those of Leon Dash in the *Washington Post* and Bill Moyers' CBS documentary "The Vanishing Family: Crisis in Black America" in early 1986 and Hodding Carter's PBS special "Crisis on Federal Street" early in 1987. When combined with such popular academic works as Charles Murray's *Losing Ground*, the effect has been to shift the focus of public discussion and policy away from the problem of joblessness or discrimination *per se* to a concern with the pathological behavior of poor people.

Many of these attacks on the Black family draw their inspiration from the pioneering work of sociologist E. Franklin Frazier. Decrying the effects of urbanization on Black family life, Frazier identified a series of negative characteristics associated with the urban, Black family. Yet, ironically, the period in which Frazier was writing, the 1930s and 1940s, is the same period sociologist William Wilson compares favorably to today's ghetto. Thus, Frazier's pathological urban family predates the rise of the social welfare policies of the sixties and undercuts the argument that government dependency is the chief cause of deviant behavior.

While the pathological model of Black family life was further elaborated by Daniel P. Moynihan in the mid sixties, the Moynihan Report and its current resurgence as a prophetic document tell us little about why some Black families succeed and others fail. In the swift response to the Moynihan Report a "resilient–adaptive" model was postulated to challenge the pathology model. This approach attempted to avoid labeling white families as normal and Black families as deviant by examining the different historical origins, cultural values and socio-economic environment of the latter.[22]

There is no controversy regarding the statistics on the Black family. While the trends for both Black and white families are generally in the same direction, there are very large gaps between the races. Since 1960 Black households have increased at almost twice the rate of white households, reflecting higher growth rates among young adults and higher marital disruption rates (resulting in two separate households). Over the last century the average household size has declined by two persons for both races (Blacks 3.0, whites 2.7).

Although fertility rates have declined for both races, Black women's fertility remains 50 per cent higher than that of white women. In 1984, 59 per cent of all Black births occurred out of wedlock compared to 13 per cent for white births. Births to Black teenagers (15 to 19) out of wedlock were four times the rate of births to white teenagers out of wedlock.

Female-headed Black families have almost tripled since 1940, reaching 44 per cent by 1985, while white families headed by a female remained stable at about 12 per cent for the period. These female-headed Black families are much more likely to live in poverty (53 per cent) than Black male-headed families (15 per cent in 1985). For whites, the comparable figures were 30 and 7 per cent.[23] Moreover, Black female-headed households are far more likely to remain in poverty over a long period.[24]

How do we explain these racial differences in family structure? William J. Wilson in *The Truly Disadvantaged* has challenged the view of conservatives like Charles Murray who argue that liberal welfare policies have enticed lower-class women to have out-of-wedlock births. Wilson contends that Black females delay marriage and have a lower rate of remarriage primarily because of the labor-market status of Black males.[25]

Although Wilson's explanation for the rise of Black female-headed households has more empirical support than Murray's it still does not fully explain Black–white difference in family structure. For example, the 1980 census data reveal that racial differences persist within income categories. It is not just at the underclass level that female-headed households are higher for Blacks but rather at every income level. The average difference between races on proportion of female-headed households is fourteen points higher for Blacks and on the proportion of husband–wife households ten points higher on average for whites.

Other residual factors like education and occupation do not eliminate this gap. Among household heads with education beyond high school for instance, 64 per cent of white households and 44 per cent of Black households are headed by couples. Only 6 per cent of these white families have female heads while 22 per cent of the Black families are female-headed. At the upper end of the occupational hierarchy, 74 per cent of white households in the executive-managerial category were husband–wife compared to 52 per cent of Black households. The figures are roughly comparable at the lower end of the occupational hierarchy with 59 per cent of Black households headed by operatives being husband–wife versus 74 per cent of white households.[26]

Reynolds Farley and Walter Allen suggest that one possible explanation for Black–white differences in family life relates to cultural norms. They have found that across various economic categories, Blacks are significantly more likely than whites to live in households that include members other than the immediate, nuclear family. This tendency also applies to Asians and Hispanics.[27] Harriette McAdoo states that the kin support network is still as essential now as it was in earlier generations. Moreover, it is as necessary to sustain one's status as it is to achieve that status. She says, "[m]obility, the result of acquisition of professional training that leads to high-paying jobs, appears to require intensive efforts by family members, and without perseverance there is a tendency to experience a decline in status."[28]

In summary, class factors do not provide a complete answer for racial differences among Black–white families. And neither does the cultural pathology model which posits an underclass value break from the middle-class norm. While it is clear that there is a correspondence between family organization and family economic status, there still remains significant variation by race in family organization. The "conventional" family model does not hold true for Black families. One might postulate that this Black redefinition and reorganization of family life has roots in both an African past and an American present. Until we examine how the Black family functions to meet its members' needs we cannot assume that changing its structure will solve the problems of its individual members.

In recent years, Asian-Americans have replaced Jews as the minority which Afro-Americans should model their behavior on. Both the popular press and scholars point to the economic success of recent Asian immigrants as evidence that racial discrimination is not a major factor in explaining the lack of Black progress. Moreover, neo-conservative scholars like Thomas Sowell argue that this success has come without the pressure of political agitation or the benefit of superior educational attainment. In short, Asian-Americans have lacked government programs like affirmative action and integrated schools but succeeded, so why can't Blacks?

Sowell attributes their success to the middle-class values of discipline, obedience, politeness, diligence, thrift, industry, hard work, and self-reliance. Starting with humble occupations, says Sowell, "these groups built businesses of 'menial' tasks and turned sweat into capital."[29] Sowell's call for a similar market orientation among Blacks ignores the historical examples of Black business and self-help leaders like Booker T. Washington and Marcus Garvey.

By basing his criteria for success on the high family income of Japanese-Americans, Sowell has opened up his interpretation to criticism. Ron Takaki has pointed out that Japanese-American families are more likely to have two income earners than are other families. In 1970, both husband and wife worked in 30 per cent of all families in the country compared to over half among Japanese-American families. The concentration of Japanese-Americans in Hawaii and California also tended to increase their income.[30]

By focusing on the success of Japanese-Americans, especially Japanese-American men, proponents of the model minority concept ignore the difficulties of other Asian immigrants to the United States. These groups often share the middle-class virtues extolled by Sowell yet make little economic progress when compared to white Americans. A study of Filipino-Americans in California by Amado Cabezas et al. states that these immigrants are among the most Westernized of all Asians with a strong family support system emphasizing the value of education and hard work. However, Filipino men, whether native or immigrant, have only about two-thirds the income of white men while Filipino women have only about one-half the income of white men. No other Asian-American group approaches parity with white men (Japanese men earn 102 per cent of the income for white males).

Immigrant Chinese-American men earn 71 per cent of the native white male norm while immigrant Korean men are at 78 per cent of the norm and immigrant Vietnamese men earn 55 per cent of native white male incomes. For immigrant Japanese-American, Chinese-American, Korean-American and Vietnemese-American women the percentages are 46, 44, 45 and 40 respectively.[31]

In part, the success of some Asians may be seen as a reflection of migration patterns. Immigration policies in the United States have generally restricted non-white immigration to relatively small numbers of professional or skilled workers. In 1965, elimination of exclusionary quotas brought a surge of largely middle-class Asian professionals from

Hong Kong, Taiwan, South Korea, India and the Philippines. After the end of the Vietnam War in 1975, 130,000 mostly middle-class refugees came to the United States. Not until 1978 did a second wave of Indochinese refugees numbering 650,000 from poor and rural areas find their way to the USA.[32] As the figures above illustrate, the success of these new citizens is far from uniform.

Wilson reports figures on "Chinatowns" that reveal 27 per cent of Chinatown housing in San Francisco is substandard compared to 10 per cent in the city at large; in Boston the infant mortality rate in Chinatown is two-and-one-half times higher than the rate for the city as a whole; and in New York 43 per cent of Chinatown families reported incomes under $4,000 annually in 1969, compared to only 21 per cent for the city as a whole. According to Wilson, the increase in immigrants has also contributed to increasing gang warfare, street crime, school dropouts and joblessness in "Chinatowns" across the nation.[33]

The failure of immigrants from diverse national backgrounds to reap the economic success of native and immigrant white males should cast doubt on the hypothesis that culture alone determines financial status. Murray's "white popular wisdom" of individual responsibility reflects hegemonic values promoted by the middle class but it does not reflect the actual choices available. That is, it does not reflect the cultural complexity found in each individual and in any given national culture.

In Nicolas Lemann's *Atlantic Monthly* piece on "The Origins of the Underclass," he contends that the roots of underclass behavior precede Great Society welfare programs. He proposes a linkage between a Southern-based sharecropper culture and underclass status in the North.[34] While Lemann offers no statistical evidence, he does recount the "ethic of dependency" that kept sharecroppers in debt and without education. He argues that the cultural dispositions of sharecroppers, furthermore, are remarkably similar to those of the underclass.[35]

Lemann's impressionistic account of rural and urban underclass society raises more questions than it answers. First, Lemann admits that some sharecropper migrants he met were successful but he says in every case they came from a two-parent home. The question remains then whether one-parent or two-parent homes were characteristic of the sharecropper culture that had an "informal attitude toward marriage and childbearing." Second, sharecroppers were employed, although the type of work resembles the underemployment found in many less developed countries. Moreover, those who migrated North came in search of industrial jobs (which Lemann acknowledges) thereby breaking any "ethic of dependency." If industrial jobs have declined in the urban areas (190,000 in 1985 alone) then it must have had an impact on underclass culture. Finally Lemann resorts to the model minority myth citing the rapid success of urban Koreans, Vietnamese and West Indians to discount economic arguments. Curiously, however, Lemann says it is because these groups maintain a separate culture that they succeed. It is not clear whether Lemann's separate culture is distinct from mainstream white culture as well as ghetto culture.[36]

Apparently, Lemann believes that at least some aspects of these separate minority cultures are good (function in a positive manner for advancement) while some aspects of mainstream culture are bad (hinder a group's advancement). For example, Sowell might suggest that mainstream culture promotes political participation, which he sees as a negative factor in minority group advancement. However, social mobility is not always the primary objective of minority group culture, especially non-immigrant minorities. Some mainstream values or alliances are rejected simply because identification with them would be identification with the "oppressor."[37]

Anthropologist John Ogbu captures some of this dynamic in his discussion of why some minorities have more difficulties with school learning than other minorities. Ogbu distinguishes between three types of minorities.

- Autonomous Minorities are minorities primarily in a numerical sense. They may have distinct cultural traits but are not politically, economically or socially subordinated, i.e. Mormons, Jews, the Amish.
- Immigrant Minorities are people who have moved to another country (e.g. US) more or less voluntarily because they believe that this will lead to better economic, political or social status. They compare themselves to peers left behind and could return to their "homeland," i.e. Vietnamese, West Indians, Italians.
- Subordinate or Caste-like Minorities are people who were initially brought into a society or country (e.g. US) involuntarily through slavery, conquest, or colonization, relegated to menial positions in society, and denied true assimilation into the mainstream of society. Their future does not look better than the past and there is generally no "homeland" to return to.

The first two groups are able to maintain a separate social identity and are not necessarily threatened that they will lose their sense of who they are. Subordinate or caste-like minorities, however, develop a sense of peoplehood or social identity that is not only different but appears to be in opposition to the social identity of the dominant group. To study in school, for example, is to act "white." If society has rejected them then they will reject society.[38]

As we move from an examination of internal explanations of under-class status to structural or external explanations, it is important to recognize the role of race. Just as most of the Office of Economic Opportunity (OEO) controversies of the sixties had a racial aspect,[39] more recent efforts to provide jobs for the underclass have involved race. Race has also played a role in limiting the availability and quality of jobs for inner-city residents.

William Wilson has suggested that the key theoretical concept in understanding underclass behavior is not culture of poverty but social isolation. Whereas the former implies the internalization of negative values and attitudes and hence policies aimed at changing these traits, the latter concept means that contact between groups of different class and/or racial backgrounds is lacking. In the case of social isolation, a public policy that broke up highly concentrated poverty areas and provided access to better schools, jobs, marriage partners and role models would be in order.[40]

For Wilson the exodus of middle- and working-class families from many ghetto neighborhoods removed an important "social buffer" that cushioned the blow of periodic recessions. In times past, these more economically stable and secure families maintained basic com-munity institutions like the church and schools and provided positive role models for those who were struggling.[41] However, Wilson over-states the degree to which the Black middle class has been able to flee the central city.

In 1970, Blacks were 4.9 per cent of the suburban population. By 1980, the Black suburban population had grown to only 6.1 per cent. Much of that growth was spillover into suburban neighborhoods adjacent to Black urban neighborhoods. In his work on the Black middle class, Bart Landry states that in three regions of the country in neighborhoods in which the majority of middle-class Blacks lived, the average probability that whites would also live there was only 20 per cent.

According to Landry, Black neighborhoods, unlike white neighbor-hoods in general, are much more class-mixed; in other words, the Black middle class will tend to reside in areas that also contain a significant proportion of Black poor and working class. In the Northeast, for example, the average percentage of middle-class Blacks in any neigh-borhood was only 38 per cent versus 62 per cent for whites. Other residents in neighborhoods where the Black middle class lived were about as likely to be from the unskilled as the skilled working class whereas there were more skilled whites in white middle-class neighborhoods.[42]

Thus the social isolation of urban Blacks is only one side of the problem of continuing housing discrimination. Landry contends "that years of living in a segregated world have distorted the consumption 'tastes' of middle-class Blacks to such an extent that their preferences remain different from middle-class whites' in many areas up to the present."[43]

Even if one is successful in breaking out of the inner city there is no guarantee that jobs will be waiting. Both middle-class and lower-class Blacks have higher unemployment rates than their white counterparts. Blacks received only 2.8 per cent of the 3.4 million new blue-collar and unskilled service jobs created between 1973 and 1981 while whites obtained 83 per cent. Landry charges that discrimination is responsible for the number of Black workers declining by 31 and 37 per cent, respectively, among unskilled laborers and domestic workers between 1973 and 1981. During the same period, unskilled Black service workers grew by 18.8 per cent compared to 26 per cent for their white counterparts.[44]

Note the following quote by Daniel P. Moynihan:

> The central conservative truth is that it is culture, not politics, that determines the success of a society. The central liberal truth is that politics can change a culture and save it from itself.[45]

If there is any truth to Senator Moynihan's proposition (and I believe there is), then two facts about our current national policy debates over the underclass seem paramount: first, the model of mainstream culture that conservatives hold dear bears little resemblance to reality; second, liberals have apparently forgotten that politics can change culture (in the larger sense of both values and economic opportunity), thereby acquiescing in the growing economic inequality of American society. The two are linked in that the cultural arguments are used to justify an economic policy that hurts the underclasses and obscures the larger cultural and economic questions.

William Wilson offers his The Truly Disadvantaged as a liberal rebuttal to the cultural arguments of conservatives. While Wilson rightly focuses on the larger questions of economic structure that affect all American workers he neglects the political issues that have divided the liberal constituency. Wilson is quick to recognize the political

advantage of universal programs that enjoy the support and commitment of a broad constituency. He contrasts favorably the New Deal
legislation of the Roosevelt administration with that of Lyndon Johnson's Great Society. These latter programs, says Wilson, fell into
disfavor because they were modeled on the English poor laws and were
increasingly perceived in narrow terms as intended for poor Blacks.[46]
Wilson, however, was not alone in recognizing the shortcomings of the
Great Society approach and the need for more basic economic planning
and reform.

   The dominant policy issue of the 1970s for the Congressional Black
Caucus was full employment. Although the 1963 March on Wash-
ington had the dual goals of "jobs and freedom" and Martin Luther
King, Jr., promoted full employment in his last book *Where Do We Go
From Here?*, the piecemeal and temporary programs of the federal
government fell far short of their objective. It was not until 1973 that
the Congressional Black Caucus, led by a representative from Watts,
Augustus Hawkins, led a long effort to update Roosevelt's original full
employment bill of 1946 and link it to both civil rights and peace.
Hawkins, joined by Senator Hubert Humphrey in 1974, introduced a
bill that stated "All adult Americans able and willing to work have the
right to equal opportunities for useful paid employment at fair rates of
compensation." To enforce this right, the bill set up a Full Employment
and National Purposes Budget, a Job Guarantee Office, a Standby Job
Corps, machinery for judicial as well as administrative appeals, local
councils to build reservoirs of public and private employment projects,
community boards, anti-inflation provisions and a prohibition against
monetary policies that would promote unemployment. Hawkins
argued that an outlay of $10 billion would create a minimum of two
million useful jobs and repay the original cost through resulting
reductions in government transfer payments and increases in the
payment of taxes to the Treasury by employed, productive workers.

   During the 1976 election campaign, Jimmy Carter refused to support
the bill on any terms. As president, he forced the extraction of the bill's
sharpest teeth – with the exception of a mandate for presidential action
to bring officially measured unemployment down to an interim goal of
4 per cent in five years. After signing the measure into law in 1978, he
promptly violated this mandate by promoting more unemployment in
the name of his failed fight against inflation.[47] One possible explanation for Carter's behavior lies in the broad range of income groups that
constitute the Democratic Party's support base. As the same time it was
gaining strength among those in the bottom third of the income scale,

new party reforms and guidelines had served to enhance the power of affluent and well-educated Democrats. As a result of these divergent tendencies economic policy was stalemated. The effect of this lack of direction and the increased mobilization of the business community set the stage for the rise of Reaganism.[48]

The Reagan administration is given credit for reducing the annual rate of inflation from 13.5 per cent to 3.6 per cent between 1980 and 1986. The price for this "economic recovery" has been sagging productivity, a lack of improvement in living standards, the serious weakness of the agricultural sector, growing numbers of the hungry and homeless, a double debt crisis – domestically and in foreign trade – and growing inequality between the rich and poor. These problems are the result not of an overly generous welfare state but rather of structural changes in the US economy.

Wilson is only one of a number of scholars to recognize that the flight of industry to the sunbelt and suburbia, the shift from goods-producing to service-producing industries, capital flight and labor-saving innovations have had a disproportionate impact on the Black labor force.[49] However, as Bertram Gross has demonstrated, the problem extends far beyond the jobless (8 million) to include job wanters and part-time employees seeking full-time work (10 million), those suffering job insecurity and low wages (36 million), and dependents of the above (108 million) for a grand total of 162 million victims of the current economic system.[50] The underclasses, especially Black males, are disproportionately hurt by the changing economy. Wilson rightly emphasizes the catastrophic nature of Black male unemployment. Only 58 per cent of all young Black adult males, 34 per cent of all Black males aged eighteen to nineteen, and 16 per cent of those aged sixteen to seventeen were employed in 1984.[51] When combined with the unusually high mortality rate and incarceration rate of Black males, the reasons for the rapidly increasing number of households headed by Black females become clearer.[52]

Wilson's case for a non-racial solution to the problem of the Black unemployed would be strengthened by an examination of the entire labor-force. One cannot ignore the fact that it was labor unions and a Democratic president that largely frustrated the economic goals of the Hawkins–Humphrey legislation.

Underlying the attack on behavior of the underclasses by what Mickey Kaus calls "the work ethic state" is the myth of the average American as a full-time worker who is secure in his or her job, satisfied with his or her wage and hopeful about advancement. Like the traditional nuclear family Moynihan advised Blacks to aspire to, "the work ethic state" holds up a model for Blacks to follow that is rapidly disappearing from mainstream culture. Full-time, year-round workers accounted for only 55 per cent of the labor-force in the United States in 1982. While it is commonly assumed that all men over the age of twenty-five are attached to the workforce, in fact, starting in their late forties and accelerating as they enter their fifties, men are increasingly leaving the labor-force. Another common assumption is that young women work for a few years and then leave the labor-force to raise a family. However, recent trends find more women remaining in the labor-force throughout their adult lives.[53]

By broadening our discussion of the underclass to include the marginally employed, the underemployed and others, we raise the concept of class in a way that is ignored by underclass theorists. Is the "underclass" to be defined solely by its relationship to work or are elements of its community life and political life important in understanding its existence? Is the "underclass" a class in itself and for itself in an orthodox Marxian sense? Is it a class that suffers from false consciousness?

Clearly, most "underclass" theorists do not see the underclass as forming a conscious group capable of fashioning a revolutionary political program. But if we accept the more Weberian view that relations in the workplace as well as residence–community relations help shape groups, the implications of using "underclass" terminology have not been explored in a productive way. If, for example, we define a class as does English historian Edward Thompson as "a very loosely defined body of people who share the same congeries of interests, social experiences, traditions and value system, who have a *disposition* to *behave* as a class, to define themselves in their actions and in their consciousness in relation to other groups of people in class ways," then the concept of the underclass as currently used has no meaning.[54]

The connection between class as objectively structured and experienced in our nation's inner-city ghettos and class as the subjective creation of attitudes and dispositions of a class or non-class kind has not been developed in the underclass debate. As long as the concept of the "underclass" is used by the dominant classes to blame poverty on the inadequacies of the poor, it will serve only a political purpose. If, on the other hand, decision-makers want to develop policies that motivate the poor and lead to self-respect they must recognize the varying subjective experiences of the poor. The "underclasses" are no more self-perpetuating than the economy is self-regulating.

Notes

1. John A. Garraty, *Unemployment in History* (New York: Harper & Row, 1978), Chapter 2.

2. The medieval standard of "reasonable and moderate" wages contrasts favorably to current workfare policies and proposals for sub-minimum wages. However, in both periods, unions/guilds seem intent on placing job security above a more general employment security.

3. See, for example, William J. Wilson, *The Truly Disadvantaged* (Chicago: University of Chicago Press, 1987); Douglas Glasgow, *The Black Underclass* (New York: Vintage Books, 1981); George Gilder, *Wealth and Poverty* (New York: Basic Books, 1981); Charles Murray, *Losing Ground* (New York: Basic Books, 1984).

4. John Iliffe, *The African Poor* (Cambridge, UK: Cambridge University Press, 1987), pp. 3–6.

5. Katherine McFate, "Defining the Underclass," *FOCUS*, vol. 15, no. 6 (Washington, DC: Joint Center for Political Studies, June 1987), p. 9. Michael Thompson and Aaron Wildavsky distinguished between poverty and destitution. They link poverty to wants, which are fixed, whereas destitution refers to needs which can be managed up and down. Their cultural theory of poverty is based on this social malleability of needs and resources. See "A Poverty of Distinction," *Policy Sciences* 19 (1986), pp. 163–99.

6. Edward C. Banfield, *The Unheavenly City* (Boston: Little, Brown & Co., 1970), pp. 125–6. Carol B. Stack has challenged Banfield's perspective in *All Our Kin* (New York: Harper & Row, 1974).

7. Creigs C. Beverly and Howard J. Stanback, "The Black Underclass: Theory and Reality," *The Black Scholar*, vol. 17, no. 5 (Sept./Oct. 1986), p. 26.

8. Ulf Hannerz, *Soulside* (New York: Columbia University Press, 1969), p. 2.

9. Ibid., p. 102.

10. Ken Auletta, *The Underclass* (New York: Vintage Books, 1983), p. xvi and p. 222. Auletta, unlike Lemann, finds distinctions between members of the underclass in the North when compared to the South. In cities, says Auletta, hostility and low tolerance for frustration seem more prevalent than in Mississippi where passivity, apathy, and low self-image are more pervasive (pp. 176–86).

11. Billy J. Tidwell, "Disaggregating Black Unemployment Status," *The Urban League Review*, vol. 10, no. 2 (Summer 1986), p. 107

12. Glasgow, *The Black Underclass*.

13. Holzer concludes that while the aspirations of Black youth equal those of white youth it is not clear whether the ability of "young Blacks" to attain their expectations is the result of lower skills, fewer contacts, less information, or simply discrimination. Harry J. Holzer, "Black Youth Nonemployment: Duration and Job Search" in Richard B. Freeman and Harry J. Holzer, eds, *The Black Youth Employment Crisis* (Chicago: University of Chicago Press, 1986), p. 65.

14. Richard B. Freeman and Harry J. Holzer in "The Black Youth Employment Crisis: Summary Finding," ibid., p. 9.

15. Ronald Ferguson and Randall Filer, "Do Better Jobs Make Better Workers?" in Freeman and Holzer, *Black Youth*, p. 291.

16. Freeman and Holzer, *Black Youth*, p. 11.

17. Kay Lehman Schlozman and Sidney Verba, *Injury to Insult* (Cambridge, Mass.: Harvard University Press, 1979), pp. 165–6.

18. Ironically Schlozman and Verba report that Blacks in the highest occupational group are the most cynical about opportunities for their children (ibid., p. 167).

19. Mickey Kaus, "The Work Ethic State," *The New Republic* (July 7, 1986), p. 22

20. Nicholas Lemann, "The Origins of the Underclass," *The Atlantic Monthly* (June 1986), p. 36.

21. Martin Kilson, "Black Social Classes and Intergenerational Poverty," *The Public Interest*, no. 64 (Summer 1981), pp. 58–78.

CHARLES P. HENRY 85

22. For a presentation of the pathology model see E. Franklin Frazier, *The Negro Family in the United States* (Chicago: University of Chicago Press, 1966); Lee Rainwater and W.L. Yancey, eds, *The Moynihan Report and the Politics of Controversy* (Cambridge, Mass.: MIT Press, 1967); and Daniel P. Moynihan, *Family and Nation* (San Diego: Harcourt Brace Jovanovich, 1986). The resilent–adaptive model is presented in Herbert G. Gutman, *The Black Family in Slavery and Freedom* (New York: Pantheon Books, 1976); Andrew Billingsly, *Black Families in White America* (Englewood Cliffs, NJ: Prentice Hall, 1968); and Carol Stack, *All Our Kin* (New York: Harper & Row, 1974).

23. Reynolds Farley and Walter R. Allen, *The Color Line and the Quality of Life in America* (New York: Russell Sage Foundation 1987), pp. 164–5.

24. Wilson, *The Truly Disadvantaged*.

25. Ibid., p. 91.

26. Farley and Allen, *The Color Line*, pp. 173–4.

27. Ibid., p. 179.

28. Harriette Pipes McAdoo, ed., *Black Families* (Beverly Hills, Calif.: Sage Publications, 1981), p. 167.

29. Thomas Sowell, *Ethnic America* (New York: William Morrow and Co., 1981).

30. Ronald Takaki, ed., *From Different Shores: Perspectives on Race and Ethnicity in America* (New York: Oxford University Press, 1987), p. 7.

31. These figures are for Asian-American groups and Native White Males in the Standard Consolidated Statistical Area of San Francisco–Oakland–San Jose in 1980. Roughly similar figures exist for the Los Angeles–Long Beach SMSA. See Amado Cabezas, Larry Hajime Shinagawa, and Gary Kawaguchi, "Philipino Americans in California in 1980: Economic Inequality from Structural Discrimination" (unpublished, UC Berkeley, 1986).

32. *TIME*, August 31, 1987, pp. 49–51.

33. Wilson, *The Truly Disadvantaged*, p. 180.

34. Lemann, "The Origins of the Underclass."

35. Ibid.

36. Ibid.

37. Lemann's references to "peasant" society and "dependency" recall the work of a number of internal colony theorists in the late 1960s and early 1970s. While some of them find their roots in Harold Cruse and Kenneth Clark, they take a very different political direction, advocating either independent Black development across class lines (right colony theory) or radical economic restructuring of the entire society (left colony theory). The internal colony model resembles dependency theory which explains Third World underdevelopment as a consequence of Western political and economic exploitation. Both approaches ignore the role of culture in minority progress. Although William Wilson's approach resembles that of the left colony theorists he ignores their work while condemning post-1965 scholarship for denying the existence of an urban underclass. See, for example, Robert Blauner, *Racial Oppression in America* (New York: Harper & Row, 1972), and Andrew Mack, et al., *Imperialism, Intervention and Development* (London: Croom Helm, 1979). Aaron Wildavsky, on the other hand, contends that economic policy in the United States is a standoff between three primary cultures of egalitarianism, collectivism and competition. It is possible to use Wildavsky's models of group culture to justify economic disparities between "Northern and Southern" countries (developed vs developing) in much the same way that neo-conservatives use cultural pathology models to justify class inequality in the United States. See Aaron Wildavsky, "Industrial Policies in American Political Cultures" in Claude E. Barfield and William Schamba, eds, *The Politics of Industrial Policy* (Washington, DC: American Enterprise Institute, 1986) and *American Political Science Review*, vol. 81 (March 1987), "Choosing Preferences by Constructing Institutions."

38. John U. Ogbu, "Minority Education in Historical Comparative Perspective," guest lecture at University of California, Berkeley, April 29, 1986. Also see John U. Ogbu, *Minority Education and Caste* (New York: Academic Press, 1978).

39. Nicholas Leman, "The Unfinished War," *Atlantic Monthly*, vol. 262, no. 6 (Dec. 1988), p. 56.

40. Wilson, *The Truly Disadvantaged*.

41. Ibid., p. 56.

42. Bart Landry, *The New Black Middle Class* (Berkeley: University of California Press, 1987), pp. 180–84.

43. Ibid., p. 80.

44. Ibid., p. 226.

45. Moynihan, *Family and Nation*, p. 214.

46. Wilson, *The Truly Disadvantaged*, pp. 118–20.

47. See Augustus F. Hawkins, "Whatever Happened to Full Employment?," *The Urban League Review*, vol. 10, no. 1 (Summer 1986), pp. 9–12.

48. Thomas Byrne Edsall, *The New Politics of Equality* (New York: W.W. Norton, 1984), p. 63.

49. See Bernard E. Anderson, "Economic Structural Change" and Linda F. Williams, "Solving the Unemployment Problem," both articles in *The Urban League Review*, vol. 10, no. 1 (Summer 1986).

50. Bertram Gross, "Quality of Life Employment," *The Nation* (November 1986).

51. Wilson, *The Truly Disadvantaged*, p. 43.

52. Daniel P. Moynihan points out that there is much less public sympathy for young Black males in the eighties than there was for the young Black victims of civil rights abuses in the sixties. From the perspective of a Bernard Goetz, they are viewed as the oppressors rather than the oppressed (*Family and Nation*, p. 215).

53. Eli Ginzberg, *Good Jobs, Bad Jobs, No Jobs* (Cambridge, Mass.: Harvard University Press, 1979).

54. Edward Thompson as quoted in Ira Katznelson, *City Trenches* (Chicago: University of Chicago Press, 1981), p. 204.

5

Blacks, Politics and the Human Service Crisis

James Jennings

Many social and economic indicators in the 1980s point to an increasingly poverty-stricken, crime-ridden, economically tenuous and growing Black America. Note, for example, that one third of all Blacks in this country live below the poverty income level of $11,000 for a family of four. In many older cities, Blacks occupy the worst housing; buildings declared unfit for human habitation decades ago are still occupied in many neighborhoods of America. It is no wonder that although comprising 12 per cent of the US population, Blacks account for 45 per cent of all deaths by fire. One out of every five Black children in America lives in officially classified substandard housing; the figure for whites is one out of ten. Black males make up 46 per cent of the US prison population. Fifty-one per cent of all Black children live in female-headed families.

Seventy-eight per cent of all white men of working age are employed; the corresponding figure for Black men is 55 per cent. Sixty per cent of white workers who were laid off between 1979 and 1983 were rehired by the same company; but only 42 per cent of Black workers were thus rehired. According to one study the "proportion of Black children below the standard grade level is 40%, compared with 23% of white children." Illiteracy among Black adults is estimated to be 44 per cent, compared to 16 per cent among whites. Forty-seven per cent of all Black seventeen-year-olds are functionally illiterate. Black children drop out of school at almost twice the rate of white children. In 1984, 27 per cent of Black US high school graduates enrolled in college, down from a high of 32 per cent in 1975. Only 8 per cent of all public school teachers are Black; in a few years this figure is expected to drop to 5 per cent. For many Blacks these kinds of problems are growing in intensity. Note further that between 1970 and 1981 the number of Black individuals living in households below the poverty level increased from 8 million to 9 million. Since 1975 the level of Black median income compared to white median income has declined to between 55 and 57 per cent. Unemployment rates for Black males and women in all age categories have increased significantly in the last twenty years.

At the same time that the Black and Latino population is growing significantly in America's largest cities, life conditions for these groups are rapidly deteriorating. The social conditions under which most Blacks live are worse today than fifteen years ago. Blacks make up a larger portion of the nation's poor today than they did at the close of the 1950s: in 1959 Blacks comprised 25 per cent of the total poor in America; by 1979 the figure was 34 per cent. Since the mid sixties, the gap between Black family and white family median income has been increasing. In 1964 the gap was $3,724; in 1979 it climbed to $8, 876. The Black teenage unemployment level has increased in recent years to between 50 and 70 per cent in many American cities. This unemployment level is considerably higher than it was ten to fifteen years ago. Generally speaking, social and economic indicators reflect a Black America which is significantly poorer and more alienated and separated from "mainstream" America than a few years ago.

Why? What are we to turn to in seeking explanations for this condition? Is it a result of lack of education? Is it a result of attitudes reflecting dependency or even laziness on the part of Blacks? Is it a vestige of slavery? Why are life conditions worsening so rapidly in Black America today? Some of this country's leading intellectuals and opinion leaders have argued or suggested that the state of Black America is a reflection of the ineducability of Blacks, or group irresponsibility, or sexual recklessness, or dependency on government largesse, or the general cultural backwardness of low-income people.

There has emerged a small but vocal and highly paid group of Black intellectuals described as "neo-conservatives" who are proposing these kinds of explanations. The ideas associated with these neo-conservatives usually go like this:

1. Race is no longer a significant variable in explaining the socio-economic mobility or living conditions found in the Black community.
2. A growing Black "underclass," with self-destructive values, is the major culprit and cause of continuing high levels of unemployment and poverty.
3. Civil Rights legislation of the '60s was effective in transforming American society into an egalitarian one; but a series of court decisions, according to neo-conservatives, also overstepped the

intent of this legislation by dictating "equality of result." But in any case, America is now in a "post-civil-rights" era.

4. Blacks of comparable educational achievement have reached income parity with whites and a vibrant Black middle class has now emerged in American society.

5. The welfare state or government cannot, and should not, attempt to be overly responsive to the social and economic problems in the Black community. This is because many conditions of social depression are a reflection of inferior culture and attitudes rather than causes which government can control.

Neo-Conservative polemic posits that attitudes of individuals are a dominant factor in determining socio-economic status. Low-income groups are characterized by negative attitudes toward work and entrepreneurship and family responsibility. This suggests that people are poor and poverty-stricken due to cultural attitudes. Some neo-conservatives go further than this: Nathan Glazer has argued that Blacks do not even have a culture, and therefore may not be able to advance themselves as was the case with other ethnic groups. As he states in his classic work, *Beyond the Melting Pot*, "It is not possible for Negroes to view themselves as other ethnic groups viewed themselves because – and this is the key to much in the Negro world – the Negro is only an American, and nothing else. He has no values and culture to guard and protect."[1] This reflects not only a flawed but also a paternalistic view of the possibility of Black economic progress and community development in American society.

The challenges are usually based on two popular propositions today; the first is that *racism is no longer a problem*. Supposedly, Blacks now have the tools to obtain improved socio-economic status, unlike the case in earlier periods. Part of this view posits that Blacks in an impoverished state are characterized as such due to lack of educational achievement, or self-motivation, and the absence of certain cultural attitudes necessary for social mobility.

In responding to the neo-conservative school, liberal policy advocates have many times utilized the same values and assumptions about race. And both liberals and neo-conservatives – whether Black or white – have overlooked the role of politics as the major explanatory factor of deteriorating life conditions for masses of Black citizens. Effectiveness of human services policies in responding to social and economic problems in Black urban communities is dependent on a number of *political* factors. The politics of social and educational services is fundamental in understanding how the current human services crisis in some Black and low-income communities developed and certainly how it can be overcome. Despite the suggestion of some neo-conservatives and liberal policy advocates that this crisis is by nature apolitical or culturally determined, the historical facts, as well as governmental actions, show that the control of various educational, economic and social processes in the Black community – and the purpose and effects of this control – are critical issues in developing strategies for resolving the human service crisis at the community level.[2]

This suggestion is not new. It is consistent with many studies investigating the social and health status of Blacks in America. That the resolution of the human service crisis in the Black community requires a political response was suggested in an official statement of the Joint Committee on Mental Health of Children a few years ago when this body pointed to the destructive effects of lingering racist attitudes:

> the racist attitude of Americans which causes and perpetuates tension is patently a most compelling health hazard. Its destructive effects severely cripple the growth and development of millions of our citizens, young and old alike. Yearly, it directly and indirectly causes more fatalities, disabilities and economic loss than any other factor.[3]

And, in a report to the National Urban League, Georgia L. McMurray identified "an emerging conservatism which encourages political leaders to limit the expansion or coverage of social programs" as one of the major reasons for the persistence of poverty and lack of food, shelter, clothing and health care in Black America.[4]

By not responding fully to the politics of human services – or even acknowledging the centrality of politics – the professional community has been ineffective in arresting the Black urban life crisis that not only continues but today is getting worse. Black urban life is deteriorating rapidly, leading one social analyst to comment that

> As American society, representing a national entity of just over two hundred years, approaches the year 2000, the social and economic conditions of American Blacks as a group reflect disturbing indications that they might become, socially and ethnically, *an endangered species*. Black social, economic, political, and cultural survival is not *guaranteed* . . .[5]

This is a serious warning considering that the social conditions under which Blacks live are worse today than ten or fifteen years ago. Blacks, as indicated above, make up a larger proportion of the nation's poor today than they did at the close of the 1950s.

The intensifying human service crisis is a direct outcome of political decisions on the part of national administrations. Worsening conditions for significant numbers of Blacks are a consequence of two factors: (1) a major political, cultural and economic assault against Blacks by private interests and the US government, and (2) a concomitant lack of political power on the part of Blacks. Between 1981 and 1984 the federal government reduced expenditures for twenty-five programs servicing children and young adults; job training was reduced by 53 per cent, mental health services by 26 per cent, the child abuse prevention program by 12 per cent and Aid to Families With Dependent Children by 18 per cent.

Lester M. Salamon, reporting for the Urban Institute in Washington, DC, stated a few years ago that these "cuts translated at local levels into losses in a number of fields, principally employment and training, housing and community development, health care outside of Medicare, and social services. Especially hard hit were programs targeted on the unemployed, on families and on children."[6] These cutbacks were not caused by the evolving Black family structure, or the educational levels of young Blacks. The cutbacks and the consequences were a result of deliberate political decisions. It was a political process which determined that Blacks and poor people would subsidize the growth of the military; in 1980 military outlays composed 23.5 per cent of the total budget, or 136 billion dollars; in 1986 military outlays composed 32.6 per cent of the total budget, or 323 billion dollars.[7]

Despite the role of politics, the importance of dedication and commitment on the part of individual professionals in the human service community should not be minimized. Neither should the efforts of persons who seek to improve, enhance and expand the delivery of ongoing human service programs in the Black community be considered insignificant. But ultimately the success of these efforts has more to do with the acquisition and maintenance of political influence and power by communities of color and their leaders than any other consideration or factor. As Theodore Cross has written in his recent voluminous work, *The Black Power Imperative*, "for all groups in a given society, the prospect for improved income, greater holdings of property, and more favorable life chances generally is profoundly influenced by the group's relationship to the instruments of power."[8] It is the level of power which Blacks can wield which determines the quality of life. The actual quality of life for the masses of Blacks has as little to do with attitudes of young Blacks as it does with the benevolence of whites.

Unfortunately, as Theodore Cross continues to argue, too many Black leaders have surrendered power for protection. Rather than developing political power, some of our liberal-minded leaders have sought to maintain government-based protection. This approach is not viable – and it never was! Black neo-conservatives have correctly pointed this out. Black people cannot rely on the good intentions of government for arresting or reversing negative living conditions. We should not forget, however, that many in the Black community have been saying this consistently – and for a long time. Martin Luther King, Jr., devoted his life to struggle because he understood that this was a necessary condition for Black progress. Malcolm X certainly did not ask Blacks to rely on government. In warning Black people not to rely on or wait for government, Black neo-conservatives are not saying anything with which there is major disagreement among Blacks. The media make it seem as if there were major disagreements about this particular point. What we will find in surveying the popular literature reflecting the thought of Black neo-conservatives is that "power" is hardly ever mentioned; it is the lack of realization of the role of power in society that convincingly separates the Black neo-conservatives from Frederick Douglass, Martin Luther King, Jr., Ella Baker, Malcolm X and others who also warned Blacks about over-relying on government or the good intentions of whites.

Black neo-conservatives hardly ever mention the need for Blacks to develop strategies of empowerment. For example, one leading Black neo-conservative has stated boldly that "clearly political power is not a necessary condition for economic advance."[9] This is naive, erroneous and ahistorical as far as ethnic groups in America are concerned. As William Ryan writes in his work *Blaming the Victim*:

> The signs are everywhere that the focus on power as the major issue is absolutely correct; the only meaningful way to [eliminate inequality] is through shifts in the distribution of power . . . the primary cause of social problems is powerlessness. The cure for powerlessness is power.[10]

A second popular argument also discourages a political diagnosis and prognosis of the human service crisis in the Black community; but it does have greater validity than the first. This explanation, however, should still not be misused as an excuse for community or governmental non-action, or as a way of blaming the victims of systematic forces depreciating the quality of urban life for Blacks. This argument posits that the socio-economic difficulties facing Blacks are a result of the rapid growth of female-headed households in this community. It is accurate – and significant – that we have a growing problem with the developing structural status of Black families. The proportion of female-headed families among Blacks has increased from 28 per cent in 1970 to 40 per cent in 1982. A single-parent family has a greater chance of being impoverished than a two-parent family. But when female-headed family comparisons are made on the basis of similar levels of education, age and region of residence, only 28.3 per cent of white female-headed families live in poverty, compared to 53.8 per cent of Black female-headed families. This suggests that something other than family structure, or perhaps in addition to family structure, explains the poverty of some Blacks. We have an obligation to question the approach of utilizing the increasing number of Black female-headed families as a scapegoat explanation for escalating poverty, especially when most white families headed by females are not impoverished. And, furthermore, the ratio of Black single-parent families to white single-parent families has actually been improving.

Arguments based on the end or decline of racism, or Black family structure, as explanations for the continual lack of economic progress for the majority of Blacks are utilized by liberals as well as neo-conservative thinkers. And both schools almost completely ignore or belittle the suggestion of greater political power controlled by Blacks as a response to the growing social and economic crisis facing increasing numbers of Blacks. One of the best examples of how the liberal school utilizes these ideas can be found in William Julius Wilson's book, *The Truly Disadvantaged*.[11] Wilson calls for a comprehensive public policy to address Black poverty that has yet to be proposed and adopted by either the Democratic or Republican parties. In his final chapter Wilson represents his public policy proposals. These include programs responding not to a culture of poverty, but rather to those social and economic forces that have produced the truly disadvantaged and the pathology associated with this status. Wilson calls for job training programs, balanced economic growth and full employment.

Despite Wilson's contributions to debates of urban poverty and race, several weaknesses remain in *The Truly Disadvantaged*. Wilson tends to de-emphasize the role of race in American society. It is one thing to show that broad economic forces and demography should be the major targets of a program for social change aimed at benefiting Blacks, rather than job discrimination on the basis of race. It is quite another thing to analyze social situations involving Blacks as if race were no longer significant.

While many intellectuals both Black and white would agree with Wilson that genuine social change must address society's fundamental economic and technological dynamics, rather than discrimination per se, many would see the denial of a racial reality in America as unfounded, to say the least. A report issued by the Atlanta-based Center for Democratic Renewal, for example, documented more than 2,900 cases of racial violence ranging from vandalism to murder between 1980 and 1986. According to some accounts the problem of racial violence has been increasing. This has led the US Congress to begin investigating racial violence under the auspices of its Judiciary Committee's subcommittee on criminal justice.

Wilson seems to be moving toward a class analysis of the social ills that he is studying. But this does not negate or run contrary to the existing racial hierarchy, which helps maintain the status quo. Wilson's implied dismissal of episodes like Howard Beach and Forsyth County, and his downplaying of continuing urban de facto segregation, reflects a lack of touch with the everyday reality of Black Americans. Wilson's view of the Black activist sector as intellectually monolithic is also problematic. Throughout the book he makes references to "Black" viewpoints without citation. It can be argued, however, that socio-economic differences within the Black community have been a major theme in writings and speeches of Black scholars and activists. In many instances Wilson's discussion of these viewpoints suggests an unfamiliarity with ongoing debates in the Black community about such issues as urban poverty, class and race.

This is typical of the ideological blindness of many "liberal" scholars who seek to discuss or explain the positions of Blacks on public issues without full knowledge of their myriad writings, speeches or scholarship and certainly without a grasp of the spectrum of ideology in the Black community. Wilson and other liberal writers may overlook this diversity because their thinking, approaches and analyses of social issues in the Black community are confined within a liberal–conservative paradigm.

Perhaps the greatest weakness of Wilson's book is his romanticism about politics. The public policy proposals which he briefly notes would indeed have a major impact on the Black underclass in some of America's cities. He is correct in calling for solutions that would seem radical compared to solutions traditionally advocated by the two national parties. But in discussing how such a program can be implemented, the author states simplistically that the agenda "for liberal policymakers is to improve the life chances of truly disadvantaged groups such as the ghetto underclass by emphasizing programs to which the more advantaged groups of all races and class backgrounds can positively relate"; this is what is referred to as the "Hidden Agenda," according to Wilson.[12]

In other words, if we can somehow couch beneficial public policy for

Blacks in ways which either do not threaten whites, or that powerful interest groups can also benefit from, we may be able to create programs to help the Black underclass. This reflects Wilson's meekness regarding class analysis. It also plays into the hands of neo-conservative thinkers who would argue that liberal public policy is keeping Blacks in a position of dependency. Wilson's liberal political solution calls for Black interests to be confined and limited by what powerful white groups may believe is in their best interests.

Wilson suggests that the problems of the truly disadvantaged may require "non-racial" solutions such as full employment, balanced economic growth, and manpower training and education. Such efforts would certainly go much further than affirmative action palliatives, but how is this political and policy transformation to be accomplished? Many of the historical and current social, cultural, and economic benefits enjoyed by whites are due to entrenched class and race hierarchies. And while some public issues can be resolved by bringing together the needs of various social sectors, many other issues are zero-sum in nature.

Wilson also speaks of broad, reform-orientated coalitions, but such coalitions will not emerge until the truly disadvantaged organize themselves politically. Many liberal (and white "leftist") scholars seem to shy away from the need for the truly disadvantaged to organize politically. This is important not only as a coalition-building tool, but also as a way for them to begin controlling those economic and social forces transforming their neighborhoods. The broad political coalition that Wilson calls for will not respond effectively to the needs of the poorer sectors of the Black community if these sectors are but "junior" political partners. Blacks must organize themselves on the basis of enhancing the quality of life in their communities, and on the basis of political equality with their potential allies in any coalition.

Wilson's book provides an excellent liberal rejoinder to the neo-conservatives. Yet despite its important contributions to ongoing public policy debates regarding race and poverty, it falls short of a complete class and racial analysis and still approaches the Black urban poor as politically incompetent.

The two major explanations of both liberal and neo-conservative policy advocates for the recent deterioration of Black urban life have to do with the deterioration of Black families, and/or cultural inadequacies. These ideas have been used as excuses for the continuation and growth of racism and "benign neglect" public policy in America on the part of both liberal and conservative administrations in the area of social services. These ideas serve as justification for continuing ineffective and inadequate policies in the area of human services in the Black community. And as in earlier periods a few well-intentioned and perhaps even mal-intentioned Black individuals have been placed in prominent positions by dominant power structures to assist in the apology and perpetuation of a racial and social order in America. These individuals do this by accepting these ideas without question or analysis, or suggesting that these issues have nothing to do with who has or does not have power in our society. Neither of these explanations or propositions appreciate the role of power, that is, of the distribution of political influence in Black urban communities. This is a critical mistake.

In fact, *it does not matter whether we intellectually decide that racism is or is not a problem; whether or not affirmative action is favored does not really matter.* And the particular family structure in the Black community could be a relatively manageable public issue if the goal were to assist people effectively. What is critical in determining the quality and level of effective human services in the Black community is the level of power which Black people can wield. It is the level of power, not IQ, genes, culture or affirmative action per se, which dictates that the majority of Blacks will live a certain way in this country.

It is the contention of this brief essay that poverty and the accompanying human service crisis is a condition which is imposed on people by the powerful in our society; it is not due to the lack of motivation on the part of Blacks or family structure. We cannot possibly develop long-range effective strategies responsive to the human service needs of Black communities by forgetting that Blacks are both racially and *politically* exploited.

Now, if this position is correct, then there are at least three responses human service providers can utilize to assist people in Black communities. These responses may not be considered political in the "electoral" sense, but they are in that they prepare clients to challenge the social and value contexts under which their receive human services. One response has to do with the raising of racial and therefore political consciousness of the clients of human service programs. The second response, related to this, is countering the negative images and messages about Blacks emanating from the media. The third response, community-controlled self-help, is most critical.

There is a growing body of evidence suggesting that racial consciousness and group pride can be an effective resource in assisting Blacks to empower themselves. This empowerment, in turn, allows Blacks to seek out the resources and networks which can be useful in meeting various educational, racial and human service needs. This has already been shown over the years, of course, through the work of groups like the Nation of Islam and other successful self-help organizations. Racial consciousness is a way of instilling confidence and motivation in youth; but it also allows the Black community greater insight in demanding and gaining greater accountability and effectiveness from institutions delivering human services. It has been reported, to use but one example of the therapeutic results of racial pride, that attitudes towards drugs have been affected for the better as racial consciousness increases. In a very important but little reported study two researchers found that social and racial consciousness are deterrents to drug abuse in the Black community.[13] Suggesting the same thing, another researcher, Elaine B. Pinderhughes, reported that cultural and racial consciousness represented important bases for social and psychological health among Blacks.[14] This kind of research suggests that those interested in increasing the effectiveness of human services in the Black community should seek to incorporate educational and social activities which raise the level of racial and cultural awareness among clients as well as facilitating their political empowerment.

Black cultural activities, as well as voter education efforts and other similar activities, require closer attention on the part of human service providers in the Black community than may be currently the case. This means that human service providers must assist parents in asserting control over schooling processes to ensure that positive messages about Blacks are being received by Black children. Research seems to suggest that institutions delivering human services should plan activities which have the effect of instilling cultural pride and sense of group history among the clients served.

It would be extremely difficult for any organization, or group seeking to increase a sense of racial consciousness, however, to do so without recognizing the great harm that mainstream media do to the Black community. Human service providers should also become more sensitive to the negative and destructive ways Blacks are treated and depicted by the media. But this too will require political action on the part of human service providers.

Admittedly, the media may seem disconnected from daily typical human service delivery-related responsibilities. Actually, this is not the case. The self-attitudes of Blacks, if negative, are not only detrimental to the well-being of the community but also quite wasteful of limited resources. One researcher reported that television entertainment inhibits the ability of Black parents to teach pride and self-respect because negative images are glamorized.[15]

Activists are emphatic in their contention that the media have adverse effects on Blacks. Dedicated and socially committed human service providers must (a) arm the Black community with information about the deleterious effects of television and radio, and (b) show the Black community how it might begin to challenge those who control the media and determine what their children and young people will be watching and listening.

Can human service professionals organize campaigns to discourage Black parents from allowing their children to watch countless hours of cultural and mental poison and self-destruction? Can we develop realistic educational alternatives for Black children who have no choice but to sit in front of a television? Are there ways to provide challenging and stimulating educational, social and recreational services during those hours when Black children are most apt to be in front of a television? Can human service providers organize Black parents to challenge local television and radio programs to be more responsive to the needs of their children? This may be more important, ultimately, than helping someone fill out an application for welfare or food stamps.

The professional Black community has a special responsibility and role in resolving the growing human crisis. Human service professionals should not allow themselves to be defined as mere bureaucrats or managers of misery. They must become an integral part of the political struggle for equality and justice in this society. What the Black community needs the most urgently in order to arrest deteriorating living conditions is the power to challenge economic, political and educational systems that have long histories of keeping Blacks "in their place." At the same time that human service professionals deliver services to their clients in the Black community there should be concomitant attempts to empower clients. Raising the racial and political consciousness of clients in the Black community and devising ways to counter the negative effects of the dominant media are but two ways by which empowerment of clients can be advanced. This empowerment, in turn, will lead to greater pressure on those with power and resources to respond to human service needs in the Black community.

It is further argued here that: (1) racism is still a fundamental problem and socio-economic dynamic in American society, and (2) until racism is eliminated through the development of Black political power, Black living conditions in this country will not improve. Black people suffer in America not because of their attitudes or sexual irresponsibility. There are indeed instances of negative attitudes and irresponsibility among individual Blacks, of course, as there are among any people, including whites in America, but to argue that Blacks are any more irresponsible or immoral than whites, and that this somehow explains poverty, broken families or unemployment, is another way of saying that Blacks are inherently inferior to whites.

The social and economic problems of Blacks in America will not be overcome until Blacks control institutions of power such as schools, banks, social agencies, health organizations and the like. It is the lack of power which allows the continuing economic and cultural exploitation of Black people. Black communities must be able to develop the wherewithal to stop or veto economic or educational processes which are imposed or are not clear about direct benefits to community residents. The political ability to stop things from occurring is not a panacea, but it is a necessary first step.

Any strategy of self-improvement which ignores the political development of Black people will not succeed. At least one lesson we can extract from the educational and economic struggles that Blacks have engaged in throughout American history is that serious economic change, beneficial to Blacks, will not occur without Blacks having the power to demand it and to politically and economically punish those who stand in the way of justice and social equality for Blacks. Political power is the key to survival for Blacks in America.

Notes

1. Nathan Glazer and Daniel P. Moynihan, *Beyond the Melting Pot: The Negroes, Puerto Ricans, Jews, Italians and Irish of New York City*, 2nd edn (Cambridge, Mass.: MIT Press, 1970) p. xxx.

2. See Edward C. Banfield, *The Unheavenly City Revisited* (Boston: Little, Brown and Co., 1974). For a recent version of this argument see Thomas Sowell, *Civil Rights: Rhetoric or Reality* (New York: William Morrow and Co., 1984).

3. *President's Commission on Mental Health*, Task Panel Reports, vol. 3 (1978), p. 822.

4. "The State of Social Services in the Black Community: A Ten-Year Perspective," *The State of Black America* (National Urban League, 1980).

5. Harold Cruse, *Plural But Equal* (New York: William Morrow and Co., 1987).

6. *New York Times*, September 1, 1985.

7. These figures are reported in Kenneth M. Dolbeare, *Democracy At Risk: The Politics of Economic Revival* (Chatham, NJ: Chatham House Publishers, Inc., 1986), p. 88.

8. Theodore Cross, *The Black Power Imperative* (New York: Faulkner Publishers, 1984), p. 15.

9. Thomas Sowell, *Civil Rights: Rhetoric or Reality* (New York: William Morrow and Co., 1984), p. 32.

10. William Ryan, *Blaming the Victim* (New York: Vintage Books, 1976), p. 250.

11. William J. Wilson, *The Truly Disadvantaged: The Inner City, the Underclass and Public Policy* (Chicago: University of Chicago Press, 1987).

12. Ibid., p. 155.

13. Lawrence Gary et al., "Some Determinants of Attitudes Toward Substance Use in an Urban Ethnic Community", *Psychological Reports* 54, 1984.

14. "Teaching Empathy: Ethnicity, Race and Power at the Cross-Cultural Treatment Interface," *The American Journal of Social Psychiatry*, vol. 4 (1984).

15. Carolyn A. Stroman, "Mass Media Effects and Black Americans," *Urban Research Review*, vol. 9, no. 4 (1984).

6

Whither the Great Neo-Conservative Experiment in New York City

Walter Stafford

This essay examines the influence of neo-conservative ideas on benefits and policies for African-Americans in New York City from 1975, the start of the fiscal crisis, to 1989. It examines the principal events that transformed New York City from the nation's most visible Great Society experiment to the nation's leading test of neo-conservative ideas. Three analytical positions of the neo-conservatives are examined in relationship to African-Americans. The first is that federally sponsored anti-poverty programs were ill conceived and were used by Black and Latino politicians to further their individual aims. Second, the conditions of poverty were moral and cultural, not institutional. Thus the welfare state was limited in making changes in the conditions of Blacks without a change in their behavior. The third was that Blacks and Latinos should not be allowed to make claims for change in institutions based on historical racism.

It is widely agreed that the emergence of conservatism as a political and intellectual force in the 1970s and 1980s was an important turning point in post-World War II American politics. Prior to the 1970s conservatives had a limited influence in the shaping of domestic policies and programs. There were influential conservatives; but no dominant ideology that shaped political life. Modern conservatism and neo-conservatism is a reaction to the epochal changes that occurred in culture, political participation and race relations in the 1960s. In one of the more unique and quixotic periods of American history, right-wing fundamentalists whose roots were in the rural South often found a common ground with urban intellectuals who were former adherents of liberal or Marxist traditions. Their common concern was the change in the traditional values that in their view undermined the family and other institutions of socialization; the growth of the welfare state and the challenges to authority resulting from the demands for political and academic participation by minorities and students.

While conservatives never achieved a political mandate from the electorate to restructure institutions, their political influence was manifested in the defeat of liberal senators who were supporters of Great Society programs and the election of Ronald Reagan in 1980.[1] These political victories amplified the appearance of a new conservative era because of the wide influence of the religious right and the intellectuals, notably the neo-conservatives. Religious fundamentalists such as the Moral Majority represented a rising influence of electronic ministries in the nation that carried political and religious messages to a wide spectrum of middle- and lower-income whites. The intellectual influence emerged from rejuvenated traditional conservatives and the neo-conservatives who operated out of academia and think-tanks such as the American Enterprise Institute, the Hoover Foundation, the Manhattan Institute and the Heritage Foundation.

The convergence of the intellectual, political and religious conservatives was a powerful alliance made even more so because of the economic decline of the 1970s. Liberalism and the Great Society programs of the 1960s were made to seem anachronistic once the nation faced recessions, inflation and greater global competition as the pre-eminent economic power. Conservatives and neo-conservatives seized the opportunity to blame many of the nation's ills, especially the decline in productivity, on a poorly motivated and poorly trained workforce that had emerged under the liberal welfare state. They also argued that centralization of concerns about equity and equal rights had usurped the powers of local governments and made the markets more inefficient. To restore the previous balance of localism and market efficiency they argued that the commitment of the federal government to equity – affirmative action programs, compensatory programs – should be weakened or eliminated.

New York City has mirrored the struggles between liberals and neo-conservatives about Great Society programs that emphasize intervention in political arrangements and economic markets. The city was one of the key sites for the program experiments of the Great Society and the intellectual response of the neo-conservatives. In both the Great Society and neo-conservative experiments the African-Americans have been central. Although African-Americans were largely excluded from the policy and program formulations of the Great Society and the intellectual analyses that were to follow, their experiences in the programs and the nature of their conditions after they ended have become one of the key areas of the debate. What made African-Americans central to the Great Society strategies was the need for the civic, political and economic elite to maintain racial and social order during the civil rights era. At stake for the elite was the stability of the social, economic and political arrangements as the city adjusted to its role in the global economy.

In the 1960s, after a period of relative political lethargy, African-Americans became a key factor and concern in the city. The riots in 1964 were the most overt manifestations of the social and economic dissatisfactions in the Black community. For the city's policy-makers the riots signaled the possibility of a protracted civil rights struggle. Although the first wave of demands of Southern Blacks in the civil rights movement for public accommodations and voting rights were not those of African-Americans in New York City, the issues in the second stage that focused on the political economy – jobs, benefits from the welfare state and institutional decision-making – struck a responsive chord among African-Americans in the city. Indeed, in terms of negotiating benefits from the welfare state, African-Americans in New York City were already at the second stage of the movement. Their problem was that they remained clients and brokers rather than decision-makers in the liberal welfare arrangements. Still, in comparison with Southern states New York had superior political arrangements for responding to the problems of African-Americans in poverty.

The relative liberalism of New York City's public and private social welfare delivery systems made it an ideal experimental site for the Great Society. New York City would become the most visible experimental ground for both theories and demonstration models in the anti-poverty programs. Cloward and Piven and their colleagues at Columbia School of Social Work provided many of the theoretical underpinnings for approaches to juvenile delinquency and welfare that were influential in the early anti-poverty strategies; the city had a network of well-educated white advocates in social welfare who had influenced the development of policies for public housing in the 1930s and helped create the prototype of youth programs, Mobilization for Youth, in the 1960s.[2] Adam Clayton Powell, the powerful Harlem Democrat, was the key leader in the House of Representatives on educational and anti-poverty programs; Black intellectuals in the city, notably Kenneth and Mamie Clark, had developed a prototype for dealing with children with psychological problems in the Northside Center and they had helped develop a format and suggested approaches for linking political, economic and educational strategies together in HARYOU-ACT; Sergeant Shriver, who was head of the Office of Economic Opportunity, was in favor of putting money into New York; the Ford Foundation saw a golden opportunity to finance experimental programs and John Lindsay, the Mayor who had won on the Liberal ticket during the initial Great Society experiment, was both committed to change and needed the resources to alter the arrangements established by the Democratic Party.

In addition to the strategic political advantages of New York City, it was also the headquarters of the NAACP and the National Urban League; CORE was still active; there were affiliates of the Student Nonviolent Coordinating Committee and the Black Panthers and Bayard Rustin, a leading theoretician, was affiliated with the unions. By the time the thrust of the Great Society programs got underway, Malcolm X had been assassinated. However, his influence was still very much alive as illustrated in the recent work by Charles Green and Basil Wilson on Black politics in New York City.[3] The creative tensions of the white liberal and African-American theoreticians and activists made New York City central to new experiments. Debates about racial integration and nationalism dominated the political discussions; bold strategies for community renewal were being devised and the opposition to change had not been mobilized.

What made the city so ripe for the Great Society experiments would also make it ripe for the neo-conservative challenge. The Great Society experiment would focus on altering the institutional arrangements that marginalized African-Americans in the labor market, education and politics. The neo-conservatives would later highlight the conflicts that emerged between African-Americans and whites as reasons why the Great Society experiment was more disruptive than helpful in the institutional planning for the poor. To understand the nature of the battle lines, it is necessary to give a brief review of the period leading up to the neo-conservative experiment.

African-Americans in New York City have historically been marginalized in the labor markets, in business and in the political arena. Although the city has the largest African-American population in the nation, they have had one of the lowest rates of business formation. The City University, which was responsible for educating many of the neo-conservatives, all but excluded African-Americans. Although New York City would develop one of the first Human Rights Commissions in 1955, African-Americans had only limited access to the government jobs that had been the source of employment for the Irish, Jews and Italians. The school system has never been responsive to African-American educational needs; and the Democratic Party had limited the ability of the few African-Americans elected to deliver benefits to their constituents. From the perspective of matching powerful liberal resources and ideas with a marginalized African-American population the anti-poverty and Great Society experiments could not have found a more favorable situation. The civic and business elite were willing to make modest compromises and the conservative and right-wing forces were poorly organized.

Under Mayor John Lindsay in the mid and late sixties African-Americans and Latinos used the anti-poverty programs to alter their role in the political structure. In 1968 an open admissions policy was initiated at the City University of New York; the school system was decentralized, leading initially to stronger demands by African-Americans for quality education of their youth; and community planning boards were developed and one of the first Community Development Corporations was created. These changes indicated modest accommodations by the civic elite. Initially they were designed not only to increase African-American participation and benefits but to maintain racial peace. Neo-conservatives like Irving Kristol supported the arrangements, as did many liberals.[4] The reasoning for the support was simple: it was much easier to accommodate participatory reforms than deal with income redistribution, better jobs and access to political and economic power. Participatory reforms were also more feasible in the view of some academicians such as Alan Altshuler (1970) because whites had no stake in who governed the ghetto. Decentralizing concessions were seen by the elite as substitutes for redistribution.[5]

It is not clear how long the civic elite thought that African-Americans would concede to their modest institutional reforms. However, it was soon clear that even the most modest concessions to African-Americans could be dangerous to a people influenced by successes in the South and Africa. It is also clear that modest concessions to African-Americans elicited unfounded fear and insecurity in white ethnic communities.

No one was quite prepared for the conflicts that would emerge from the 1960s experiments in New York. Even relatively minor institutional change that was perceived as favoring African-Americans or Latinos weakened the coalitions with Liberals in New York and set the stage for galvanizing coalitions or conservatives.

Four examples among the many that occurred in the period are reviewed here. The first was the conflicts that emerged in the anti-poverty programs. Unquestionably, the choice of New York City as the most visible site for the Great Society programs had its benefits. Head Start, legal service, health and job training programs were initiated in this period. African-Americans, however, had largely been excluded from the development and planning of the programs and from their administration. They were the field soldiers. With the increasing radicalization of the African-American community and their view that they had the ability to control and administer the anti-poverty programs, a struggle emerged with whites for administrative and policy control. Following escalating tensions from their picketing of the administrative offices, the African-Americans wrestled control of the administration.[6] The control of the anti-poverty programs provided African-Americans one of the first opportunities to expand their political base independent of the parties and assume the position of leaders around issues of poverty. It also served as a fulcrum for increasing managers in the fragile middle class.

In the arena of the public schools, the decentralizing activities were numerous but the most notable was Ocean-Hill Brownsville in which the African-American Teachers' Association was an active influence in establishing policies and programs for community control. A crisis emerged in 1968 when the African-American parents and teachers came into conflict with the predominantly white United Federation of Teachers. A white administrator had been in line for the superintendent position but parents elected to support a Black educator who in turn appointed five minority principals. These appointments angered both the UFT and the Board of Education.

In the turmoil that followed the UFT attempted to undermine the Black administrators. When the latter refused to readmit the teachers, the UFT went on strike, leaving only 140 Black teachers available to keep the entire district functioning. Ultimately the strike was settled and a decentralization bill passed by the state legislature favorable to the union. However, in the deals that were subsequently negotiated the key Black administrators were politically isolated and left the school system. The Afro-American Teachers' Association survived only four more years.[7]

In addition to the conflicts in the schools and the anti-poverty programs, African-Americans and their allies attempted to get a civilian complaint review board to deal with the numerous cases of police violence against Blacks. Lindsay created a Civilian Review Board in which the majority of the members were citizens. The Patrolmen's Benevolent Association (PBA) joined with other conservative forces in the city and placed the issue on the ballot. Less than 40 per cent of the voters supported the creation of a civilian review board.

And finally, Mayor Lindsay attempted to develop scatter-site housing for the burgeoning segregated African-American communities. The sites selected for the housing were in Forest Hills, a predominantly white community in the borough of Queens. Whites in Forest Hills opposed the site selection plans and the issue became one of the most volatile discussions about racial integration in the city and nation. The Forest Hills episode showed that Lindsay's vision of an integrated city was beyond that of many of his allies in the liberal coalition. By the early 1970s the implicit message from the liberal coalition and the business and political elite was that minor forms of decentralization could be supported; but major shifts in power and territorial changes would not.

All the issues that had been simmering in the Great Society years would come to a head in 1975 when the city faced bankruptcy. Many academicians and social critics would charge that a major reason for the city's fiscal crisis was its attempt to meet the demands of African-Americans and Latinos, most notably the expansion of welfare payments for Open Admissions and costs for services.

By the time of the fiscal crisis, African-Americans were fighting brush fires in almost every issue area. The national mood was becoming more conservative and the civil rights movement had waned. Although Mayor Abraham Beame, who succeeded Lindsay, kept many of Lindsay's staff members and appointed the first and only African-American to head the Human Resources Agency, which had been the source of tensions between African-Americans and white social service agencies, the liberal Great Society period was nearing an end. The conservative forces did not exactly have a cake walk; but it was close to it. Looming in the background during this period were some of the most powerful corporate and intellectual forces in the nation. No African-American community would have been able to withstand the conservative influences, and certainly not New York's Black community. By the fiscal crisis Black radicals had been isolated or co-opted into the community and educational boards and the anti-poverty programs; only a few of the potential city-wide African-American advocate groups remained; Black managers and officials in the anti-poverty and civil rights organizations were being hired in the first wave of community development officers in the corporate sector; the national civil rights movement had petered out and there were lingering tensions between Blacks and Jews in the city because of the anti-poverty and school decentralization issues.

The fiscal crisis marked a turning point in New York City politics because it brought the confluence of conservative forces galvanized by local and national events around race relations together. This would prove a major setback for African-Americans and force their advocacy and policy recommendations in the future into the political center.

Indeed for the next decade only a few city-wide advocate groups among African-Americans would emerge and none would be widely effective. Homelessness, joblessness, police violence and racially motivated attacks increased rapidly.

With the election of Edward Koch in 1977 political and policy conservatism found a new platform. First, financial interests pressured city officials to retrench city government which set back the gains that had been made by African-Amerians and Latinos, tuition fees were raised at the formerly free City University and the state imposed controls with businessmen as overseers.[8] The corporate interests led by David Rockefeller also organized the New York City Partnership in 1979. This coalition included some major global industries. In a short period of time they would emerge as a leading barometer of how the corporate interests decided a big city should be managed.

In 1977 Edward Koch, who ran on a law and order platform, opposed the scatter-site housing proposals of the Lindsay administration and promised to bring economic viability to the city, was elected. Mayor Koch focused his political agenda on representing the upper-income and white working-class constituents and taking on Black politicians and activists who had gained a political foothold in the Lindsay era. He was the quintessential messenger of the market-place. The white civic elite and the city's liberal dailies may have been offended by some of his racial comments. However, as Shefter notes, almost all sectors were ready to beat back the demands for institutional change occurring in the African-American community.[9] Almost no one, including most of the white allies of African-Americans, was ready to openly challenge the new arrangements.

Mayor Koch was only one cog in the new neo-conservative wheel, but he was an important one. In him, the neo-conservatives had one of the nation's most influential politicians espousing their ideas and concepts. Aside from Ronald Reagan Mayor Koch was probably the politician who received most attention for his support of neo-conservative ideas. During his tenure he was the nation's best-known mayor and his two books were on the bestseller lists.[10] The books were witty and insightful examinations of his views on the city, politics, and Blacks. In them, Koch writes of his opposition to quotas, set-aside programs and many of the anti-poverty programs; his support for the death penalty, even before he was elected mayor, and his strong misgivings about approaches advocated by African-Americans for political and economic change.

Mayor Koch altered the rules that had been established between white and Black politicians by questioning whether Black politicians who branded him racist knew what was in the best interest of their constituents. According to Shefter, this broke a long-standing tacit agreement in the city that white politicians would remain mute when Black politicians denounced them for racism, thereby allowing Black politicians to retain the support of their followers even when they were obligated to accept compromises that left their constituents at the bottom of the social and economic ladder.[11] He also demeaned African-American culture and traditions. Despite his claim of support for the tactics of the Southern civil rights movement – Koch worked briefly in Mississippi during the movement – he had Black ministers arrested for organizing a sit-in at City Hall. Despite his claim of sensitivity to racial matters and stereotypes, Mayor Koch donned an Afro-wig and mimicked Blacks at a social event.

The fiscal crisis provided the opportunity that the neo-conservative intellectuals needed to promote their ideas for restructuring the city. Many of the neo-conservative ideas from New York City read like a section from an American who's who of intellectualism. Most notable among the names are Nathan Glazer, Irving Kristol, Norman Podhoretz, Roger Starr, Daniel Moynihan, Seymour Martin Lipset and Daniel Bell. Although there are a large number of prominent neo-conservative scholars who are not from New York City, such as Edward C. Banfield, James Q. Wilson and others, it was the New Yorkers who largely set the tone of neo-conservatism.[12]

These supporters of the New Deal became assiduous critics of the Great Society Programs. These graduates of the free City College questioned the advisability of Open Admissions, questioning not only the intellectual ability of Black and Latino students but the very survival of the university. The neo-conservatives argued against affirmative action, proposing that "merit" should be the sole criterion for access and mobility. Although this group was diverse collectively they emerged as some of the nation's most influential intellectuals. Their ability to influence the mass media, but especially conservative politicians and businessmen on race relations, was undisputed.

The neo-conservative intellectuals filled a vacuum created by the fiscal crisis and the conceptual crisis around race relations as well. Following the civil rights movement, academicians had been at an impasse about the framework for analyzing race relations. Many of the neo-conservatives, notably Moynihan and Glazer, had been promoters of the thesis that the decimation of the Black family with all its attendant social pathologies was the major reason for the absence of Black progress.[13] The ideas of social pathology were attractive to journalists and commentators. The neo-conservatives are responsible for promoting the idea that the culture of Blacks, including their morals and family traditions, are the reasons for the economic problems of Blacks; they have argued that culture limitations of Blacks are one of the reasons they have not become as assimilated as other immigrant groups and they have revived or at least kept alive the notions of Blacks' criminal proclivities. Their frame of reference is distinctly urban, and their conceptual framework is the immigrant analogy – a variation of the melting-pot theory – which is a distinctive New York City assessment of race and ethnic relations that is still proposed in neo-conservative literature.

The pervasiveness of the ideas about a culture of poverty in New York were reflected in the books and articles by journalists, academicians and governmental planners. The first wave of the new underclass theories emerged from the city in the book published by journalist Ken Auletta.[14] As more academicians joined the consensus, notably Blacks, including liberal William J. Wilson and neo-conservative Glen Loury, their framework often seemed irreproachable.[15] Although criticisms of the underclass concept gradually emerged, over the course of the 1980s the neo-conservatives would influence social welfare pursued by New York State.

An example of the neo-conservative underclass influence was the Commission on the Year 2000. In 1985 Mayor Koch convened representatives of the civic elite, including three Blacks – the former Director of the New York Urban League, a nationally known scholar and the Commissioner of the Human Rights Commission – to examine the prospects and problems facing the city in the twenty-first century. Although the civic members may not have been neo-conservatives, the Commission's reliance on the underclass concepts of William J. Wilson and the choice of Nathan Glazer and Roger Starr as two of the principal researchers certainly gave its final report a decisively neo-conservative tone. The document, New York Ascendant, barely addresses the racial conflict in the city and relies heavily on the use of the immigrant analogy when explaining the slow progress of African-Americans in the city.

In addition to the persuasive influence of the neo-conservatives through journals and their positions of power, they also had the benefit of a leading think-tank. New York City is one of the few cities, if not the only city, where a leading conservative think-tank, the Manhattan Institute, has focused on local problems and disseminated and organized seminars for businessmen. The Manhattan Institute was established in 1978 by William Casey, former Director of the Central Intelligence Agency. It has been responsible for funding some of the most

influential books on social and racial policy, including George Gilder's
Wealth and Poverty and *Losing Ground* by Charles Murray.[16]

Gilder's argument parallels those of the white and African-American
neo-conservatives. He argues that while slavery had been responsible
for the historical inequality between Blacks and whites, the civil rights
laws of the 1960s changed the political and economic climate. According to Gilder the nation is now in an era of post-racism where forces
other than historical discrimination must account for the persistence of
poverty amongst Blacks. Gilder's explanation for the malaise facing
Blacks is that liberalism, especially the Great Society programs, led to a
rise in female-headed households. His solution is for the government to
minimize its intervention in the market and for Blacks to break away
from the inhibiting welfare programs.

In *Losing Ground* Murray acknowledged that race relations was the
critical problem in social policy and that no serious welfare reforms
could be accomplished without addressing it directly. However, like
Gilder, Murray relies on the argument that the culture of Blacks and the
programs of the 1960s were the real culprits of African-American
problems. In Murray's view the insularity of the Black poor, along with
their low self-expectations and inability to assume responsibility for
their actions, were the critical problems.

In addition to these national bestsellers, the Manhattan Institute has
also published a widely circulated book, *New York Unbound*, on New
York City, where conservative and neo-conservative authors, including
Nathan Glazer and Roger Starr, presented their arguments on poverty,
welfare and housing in the city.[17] The principal argument of the book is
that five factors forced New York City to become "unbound." They
are: fear of the market-place; New Yorkers' pursuit of a free lunch; the
propensity to regulate; the vested interests; and indifference to the
impact of taxation. The authors pined for an unbridled market-place
and for change in the behavior of the welfare class. Like the dominant
conservative ethos of the era they praised the newly arriving Asians for
their capitalist spirit.

A decade after the fiscal crisis the African-American community was
in dire straits. At the beginning of the fiscal crisis, their unemployment
rates had been similar to those of whites. By 1985, they were two and a
half times as high. Homelessness had increased to a point that African-
American men could be seen begging at almost every subway station in
Manhattan. Arrests of Black men had increased to the level that over 70
per cent of the inmates in New York State prisons were Black and
Latino men. Racially related violence by citizens and police increased.
Between 1980 and 1986 New York City had more racially related

murders by white mobs than Los Angeles and Chicago combined and there were increasing deaths of African-Americans in police custody.

As events worsened for African-Americans in the 1980s there were virtually no institutional mechanisms for them to respond politically to Mayor Koch. Although he appointed the first Black Chief of the Police Department and he was always able to find accommodating Blacks to serve as assistants and commissioners, he continually alienated the African-American community. *The Amsterdam News*, a weekly African-American paper, kept a front-page editorial running that "Koch must go." Nevertheless, despite the alienation of African-Americans from City Hall, they exercised few options in dealing with Koch in the early years. Mayor Koch received a large segment of the Black vote in his first and second terms for office.

As a result of the weak African-American opposition and the growing power of the conservatives, Mayor Koch implemented neo-conservative policies with impunity. With an African-American deputy mayor in front charging that the anti-poverty programs were corrupt and run by "poverty-pimps," he wrested control of them from African-Americans and Latinos and centralized them in his office. He refused to even consider the drafting and implementation of a public sector affirmative action program, making New York City the only major locality without one. Despite the small number of Black businesses, he refused to establish a set-aside program.

The major problem in the African-American community was finding ways to regroup organizationally. By wresting away control of the anti-poverty programs, Mayor Koch weakened the prospects for African-Americans to organize around the issues of jobs, homelessness, education or violence. As a result, although the social and economic problems of African-Americans accelerated in the city, no city-wide coalitions were sustained to deal with them. Unlike the 1960s and 1970s, the regrouping process that occurred among the African-American community was no longer around nationalism and institutional control.

Reflecting the national trends of the Black middle class brokering for positions in the margins of the private sector and in the welfare state, African-Americans created such organizations as the 100 Black Men and 100 Black Women. The leaders of these two organizations were often invited to meetings when crises emerged. However, they wielded only limited influence or impact in altering the balance of power in the city. Their primary successes were to obtain jobs for individual members of the organization and make white policy-makers aware of the presence of a politically active Black middle class.

Attempts in the African-American community to focus on cultural and politicized Black nationalism were often fraught with difficulties. Although another African-American teachers' organization emerged to supplant the organization disbanded after Ocean-Hill Brownsville, their leaders were often isolated in the conservative Black and white communities.

In addition to the civic and professional groups, and the Black nationalists, there were an increasing number of Black elected officials in the city council and in the state legislature. However, in a weak city council, the Black members were virtually impotent and few of them were strong advocates of programs and issues for African-Americans. Indeed, in the city council, the issues around affirmative action were kept alive largely by white women.

Some Blacks in the state legislature were very effective in raising important issues. Al Vann, a leader in the Ocean-Hill Brownsville dispute, was an important advocate around issues for children. Roger Green, also from Brooklyn, was largely responsible for creating the Center for Law and Social Justice in Brooklyn that became one of the two leading organizations in the city advocating and monitoring issues around police violence, joblessness and resources.

Finally, the African-American community invested its emotional and political energies in David Dinkins, a tireless candidate for office who won the Manhattan Borough presidency in 1985. This was the first time that a Black held the seat since 1975 and along with the Center for Law and Social Justice the African-American community finally had two well staffed agencies that could advocate for their needs. Dinkins assembled an effective racially integrated staff that worked as advocates and monitored the distribution of city funds. In 1989, he defeated Koch in the Democratic Primary.

As important as this event was, the defeat of Mayor Koch in 1989 represented the removal of only one wheel in a powerful conservative train. During the Koch administration African-Americans had fallen behind their brothers and sisters in almost every other major urban area in terms of social and economic indicators. New York City was the only major city in the nation without a public sector affirmative action program; the city never developed a set-aside program for Black businesses; African-Americans received less than one per cent of the nearly 6 billion dollars spent on goods and services in 1986; the city had not developed any linkage programs that committed the corporate sector to community economic development for low-income residents, and although Blacks gained tin-city jobs they largely remained segmented in a few agencies.

One of the interesting outcomes of the neo-conservative experiment was the unwillingness of African-Americans to deal with issues that might be considered politically to the left. This had several consequences. First, it left the advocacy for almost all major social and economic issues in the hands of whites. Although the white advocates are well educated and effective researchers and lobbyists, they cannot legitimately raise issues about racism on a consistent basis. New York City is probably one of the few cities where white intelligentsia represent the thinking, actions and values of African-Americans without the input of this very same group! Following the fiscal crisis the white academic community wrote articles about the city that largely focused on efficiency. Indeed, as noted previously, some white academicians hypothesized that it was the city's attempt to deal with demands made by African-Americans in the 1960s that led to the fiscal crisis. Few white academicians linked the issues of poverty and racial discrimination to the problems that were emerging in the city and African-Americans produced few documents to counter white interpretations. Despite the presence of several Black presidents in the City University of New York and a scattering of African-American study programs in the public and private universities, there were few documents produced by African-Americans on the city.

The isolation of the African-American left meant that the issues and the programs that they raised were often dismissed as disruptive of the new arrangements. Interestingly, the programs and ideas raised by the Black left were actually "centrist" in the sense that policies advocated have been adopted by government in other cities. They mobilized to stop police violence, demanded an affirmative action plan, requested that the European focus of the teachers be replaced by a multi-racial ethnic framework and raised issues about community economic development. From a broader perspective the African-American experience in the city has to be seen as part of a analytical scenario that includes the emergence of a "neo-conservative" version of the welfare state. Under the credo of the conservative welfare state all interests must pull together to avoid crises. Following the fiscal crisis the civic, business, academic and political elite defined all issues in terms of the city's recovery. Either a group was for the recovery or against it. They promoted the generalization that all groups would benefit with a revitalized economic base and they created levels at which groups could discuss their dissatisfactions with new arrangements.

Under the neo-conservative welfare state, the issues among African-Americans in the city have often become how and who brokers for benefits to lower-income blacks. Blacks who advocate change in the arrangements are excluded from the new alignment of Black brokers and almost certainly from contact with the white elite. The new African-American brokers usually have little influence in the larger African-American community. Their lack of a community-based connection is a benefit to the elite; Black brokers are used by the elite as sounding boards to determine which organizations should be funded, or isolated.

In the new conservative arrangements, the white civic elite has largely removed itself from the issues of poverty and welfare. They have followed the direction of the white technicians and academicians, who have defined the city's problem in terms of efficiency. The few African-Americans who participate in these circles are pacified or isolated. The economic elite in the neo-conservative experiment are elated to have relative racial peace and the support of an intellectual class. Through their partnership they can use their relationships and resources to influence outcomes of economic and political events. Through their connections with the media and as overseers of the city's financial control boards they can anticipate and recommend policies to limit future crises, and continue to control the politics, and political future, of African-Americans.

Notes

1. Examples of liberal US senators defeated by conservatives during the last twenty years include Frank Church of Idaho, Burch Bayh of Indiana, and John Culver of Iowa.

2. See Daniel P. Moynihan, *Maximum Feasible Misunderstanding* (New York: The Free Press, 1970).

3. Charles Green and Basil Wilson, *The Struggle for Black Empowerment in New York City* (New York: Praeger, 1989).

4. Irving Kristol, "Decentralization for What?," *The Public Interest*, no. 11 (Spring 1968); see also Ira Katznelson, *City Trenches: Urban Politics and the Patterning of Class in the United States* (Chicago: University of Chicago Press, 1981).

5. Alan Altschuler, *Community Control: The Black Demand for Participation in Large American Cities* (New York: Praeger, 1970).

6. Charles Morris, *The Cost of Good Intentions* (New York: Norton, 1980).

7. Green and Wilson, *The Struggle for Black Empowerment*.

8. Robert Pecorella, "Fiscal Crises and Regime Change: A Contextual Approach" in Haywood Sanders and Clarence Stone, eds, *The Politics of Urban Development* (Lawrence, Kan.: University of Kansas Press, 1987); see also Martin Shefter, *Political/ Fiscal Crisis: The Collapse and Revival of New York* (New York: Basic Books, 1985).

9. Shefter, *Political/Fiscal Crisis*.

10. Edward Koch, *Mayor* (New York: Warner Books, 1984); and *Politics* (New York: Warner Books, 1986).

11. Shefter, *Political/Fiscal Crisis*.

12. Peter Stenfels, *The Neo-Conservatives* (New York: Simon and Schuster, 1979); and Alan Wald, *The New York Intellectuals* (Chapel Hill: University of North Carolina Press, 1987).

13. See Daniel P. Moynihan and Nathan Glazer, *Beyond the Melting Pot* (Cambridge, Mass.: MIT Press, 1970).

14. Ken Auletta, *The Underclass* (New York: Random House, 1982).

15. See Glen Loury, "A New American Dilemma," *The New Republic* (December 31, 1984), pp. 14–18.

16. George Gilder, *Wealth and Poverty* (New York: Basic Books, 1984); and Charles Murray, *Losing Ground: American Social Policy 1950–1980* (New York: Basic Books, 1984).

17. Peter Salins, *New York Unbound* (New York: Basil Blackwell, 1988).

7

Race and Economic Development: The Need for a Black Agenda

William Fletcher and Eugene Newport

The crisis threatening Afro-America is not simply that there is Black poverty. Rather it centers around the chronic nature of that poverty and some of the structural changes currently underway which may institutionalize a deepening of that situation. Further evidence of the crisis is summarized in the following indicator:

> The number of middle-income male jobs, those paying between 125 and 75 percent of the median male earnings, declined from 23.4 to 19.7 percent of all jobs between 1976 and 1984. And we now have more than two million people working full time all year who still fall below the poverty level. One out of every five husbands heading two-parent families and two-thirds of all women heading single-parent families do not make enough to lift a family of four out of poverty.[1]

The "hollowing" of the US economy with the decline in manufacturing in the industrial base – along with the corresponding rise in the service sector and its depressed wages – has created a situation which some commentators describe as the foundation for the Black "underclass." The elimination of solid manufacturing jobs from the so-called "rust belt" has had a profound impact on African-Americans. Blue-collar employment in manufacturing was one important means for Black workers to gain semi-skilled and later skilled employment commensurate with a "liveable" wage. *Business Week* noted, for example: "The pay gap between industrial and service sector workers remains wide: Average hourly pay is 11% lower in services in the private sector than in manufacturing."[2] In concrete terms, consider the following: "The average pay in the health services industry, which generated 1.2 million jobs during those years [1981–87] was only $23,000, while salaries in the retail trades, which generated the most jobs – 3.4 million – averaged only $13,000."[3] Additionally, many of these same jobs were unionized, resulting in substantially higher income than similar non-union employment. With the shift of these production facilities off-shore or their closure entirely the opportunities which were once there evaporated. The current crisis in Black living conditions calls for the development of new political and economic strategies. It is this realization that has spurred the call for a new "Black agenda."

A debate is taking place within Afro-America surrounding what is referred to as a "Black agenda." On the national level this has been represented in part by the 1989 New Orleans African-American Summit. This kind of effort has a long historical precedent, not only in recent conferences and summits (for example, National Black United Front, National Black Political Assembly, Little Rock National Black Political Convention, and so on) but much earlier than these particular events. The first National Negro Convention was held in Philadelphia in 1830 and addressed itself to devising "ways and means for the bettering of our condition." Subsequent to the Philadelphia gathering, other such meetings were held through 1865. These periodic gatherings were more sparsely held after this period.

The current demand for a Black Agenda, on both the local and national level, reflects in part the beginning of a new political movement. Such a view is supported by other developments such as the local electoral surges that reflected Black resistance to Reaganism for a large part of the 1980s, as well as the two Jesse Jackson presidential campaigns. But the call for a Black agenda also reflects a deepening social and economic crisis in Black America that neither liberals nor neo-conservatives have been able to respond to effectively.

The factors leading to the demand for a Black agenda would not be complete without adding the impact of Reaganism and the uncertainty regarding the future under Bush. Reaganism had a demonstrable negative effect on the living standard of African-Americans.[4] The additional impact of Reaganism was its disorganizing affect on pro-gressive social forces and its explicit and implicit support for various reactionary movements and tendencies. It is to the credit of Afro-America that it can claim to have led the main resistance to Reaganism. Nevertheless, Afro-America did not escape the ideological impact of Reaganism, a point which we shall clarify below.

Though Reaganism represented a major setback for progressive social causes and movements, it did not succeed in creating a lasting realignment as its namesake and ideologues prophesied. Reagan proved to have no demonstrable coat-tail effect, and as popular a person as he was, his specific policies generally met with a less than enthusiastic response from the population. The lack of realignment can also be seen in the ambivalent attitude in the ruling circles regarding George Bush, perhaps exemplified by the drop in the stock market the day following the election. As early as the 1984 elections it became clear that there was little political coat-tail effect for Republicans in the wake of Reagan's defeat of Mondale. Later, in the 1986 mid-term elections, the Republicans suffered an even more significant defeat, losing control of the Senate. Contrary to the juggernaut image of the early Reaganism, it became clear by his second term that there was neither a realignment nor a solid ruling-class consensus in favor of his policies and practices. Discussions during the first "hundred days" of the Bush administration regarding inconsistencies and lack of policy reflect both on Bush the man, and also on Bush as the successor in Reagan's attempted "counter-revolution."

This period of lack of clarity also impels the need for a common African-American approach to the next period. The disarray in the ruling political circles has not, however, translated into clear and operative unity on the ground. Indeed, one impact of Reaganism has been to sharpen differences *within* the African-American community.

In order to understand the differences, it is essential to examine the struggle between classes within Afro-America. Within this contest the role of the Black middle class is critical. Defining the "Black middle class" is perhaps the first and most difficult exercise in any such discussion. For the purposes of this essay, we are not referring to income. We are rather referring to that group (and its political representatives) which have an existence as a professional, managerial, and/ or small-business strata. Included within this grouping are lawyers, doctors, realtors of large multi-family dwellings, ministers and corporate managers. Due to the fact that there is only a limited "bourgeoisie" to speak of among African-Americans, we will also include venture capitalists, bankers and owners of some of the larger Black businesses within this category, only for the purposes of discussion.[5]

A Black professional and entrepreneurial stratum has existed since before Emancipation. Subsequent to the Civil War this stratum attempted to give leadership to the rest of the African-American people. Substantive differences developed over direction, however, in part brought on by the collapse of Reconstruction. A few brief points are worth noting. First, there always existed a tension in terms of the question of economic development. With the defeat of Reconstruction and the massive setbacks in the political status of African-Americans, the Black middle class grew within the context of the Jim Crow, segregationist South. In doing so, its development was distorted. The Black middle class could only grow where white America decided not to tread in order to avoid inter-racial contact on the basis of business interests. Examples of this include mortuaries, insurance companies serving Blacks, banks and cosmetics. But entry into the field of heavy industry (for example, steel) was out of the question.

Second, the Black middle class was not only excluded from important sections of the economy, but it was also geographically restricted in terms of places to live. This point has become the subject of much discussion recently with some observers, such as William Wilson, attributing the depressed state of the Black communities to the flight of the Black middle class.

The social, political and economic restriction of the Black middle class gave rise to diverse strategies for liberation and development. One important characteristic of the ensuing debates was the manner in which the class demands of the Black middle class were generally framed within the context of the battle for basic Black freedoms. Thus, what we refer to as the civil rights movement often sponsored demands for justice and equality through the prism and screening of Black middle-class elements.

The breakdown of the "civil rights" consensus and the dilemma facing the Black middle class can be seen as resulting from several factors. Victories in civil rights legislation and judicial decisions shattered many prior barriers to economic and social development. Corporate America, as a matter of fact, began to perceive potential new and lucrative markets in Afro-America in the areas of cosmetics, insurance and automobiles. This threatened the Black business base. These Black businesses, however, could not seek to raid white communities for consumers for whites would not patronize them.

The end of legal segregation and the disruption of the African-American market also threw into disarray many of the political organizations which spoke for the traditional middle class. Groups like the NAACP were not quick to respond to the crisis and developments facing the traditional middle class, nor did they loyally speak for the upwardly mobile sector. Newer formations came into existence to respond to this crisis and herald Black economic development. Operation PUSH, founded and led by the Rev. Jesse Jackson, perhaps typified this phenomenon. Groupings such as PUSH walked the line between playing the role of intermediaries for corporate America and at the same time promoting visions of self-reliant developments (for example, Jackson's all-but-forgotten "kingdom theory").

The new sector of the Black middle class thus arose as both "children" of the victories of the 1960s as well as being those who served the newly developing industries such as information processing and financial management. This sector exists as one leg of the base of Black neo-conservatism. The other leg of Black neo-conservatism is a reactionary, virulently anti-community and homophobic sector of the fundamentalist Black clergy which has responded to the ideological and political vacuum in Afro-America with a set of "traditional" values very much consistent with aspects of Reaganism.

In Boston the development of a political process to produce a Black agenda reflects some of the dynamics described here. Representatives of community agencies, area politicians, the clergy, academia and several community activists gathered together to discuss the question of a Black agenda. Though not representing all sections of the community, this and similar gatherings around the USA represent more than the search for proverbial Black unity. These gatherings are hoping to provide a response to the leadership void within the Black people's movement and respond to the social and economic crisis gripping Afro-America as a whole.

Symptomatic of this and other similar gatherings is the lack of a qualitative interchange between the alleged leadership and the mass base. Indeed, while this grouping attempts to adopt or construct a Black agenda, it does so with inconsistent attention to community-wide discussion. For some of the participants this effort is one step toward reassuring themselves that they *are* the community's leadership, despite opinion polls which demonstrate that, in Boston at least, the community believes that to the extent to which it has a leadership, that leadership resides among local community activists.

This perhaps cynical portrayal of local efforts at the development of a Black agenda is not aimed at dismissing it. Rather it seeks to illustrate the ambiguous role which efforts at a Black agenda play at this point. In one sense, Black agenda efforts represent something old and something new. The something "old" are the old-line Black leadership, some of whom head community agencies, who face the destruction of their institutions and corresponding role in the community. The local efforts of Boston's Black Agenda Project are based on providing progressive leadership for African-Americans. This forces them to come into conflict with white corporate America and those forces grouped around Reaganite and reactionary policies.

The something new, however, is not necessarily something "good." A more self-conscious element of the Black middle class seeks hegemony. Groups such as Boston's Minority Developers' Association have arisen which seek to articulate a conception of Black community development which is shaped by the needs and demands of the Black middle class.

The other new factor is the participation of a clear progressive trend from within the African-American movement. This trend, much of which became self-conscious and invigorated by the Jackson presidential campaigns, is loosely grouped. Not existing as a specific organization, and encompassing a variety of political views ranging from Marxist to religious nationalist, what this grouping has in common is its attention to: (1) involvement of grassroots Black people in producing an agenda; (2) an anti-corporate, anti-imperialist orientation; (3) a conception of community development which is collectivist in orientation rather than individualist.

Those activists identifying with these three ideas find themselves in contention for leadership of the community. This situation, which encompasses major tensions and contradictions in the pursuit of political and economic empowerment in the Black community, provides evidence for the limitations of the Black middle class and coalition building articulated in the early 1970s. Those sections of the Black middle class which are feeling crushed by "fiscal conservatism" are floundering and being pulled in different directions. Agency directors, for example, while perhaps having hoped for the role of "intermediary" between corporate America and Afro-America, are witnessing their agencies being whittled away. This leads some to fight, while others choose alternative paths of collaboration.

The issue of economic development has in this situation become one important piece of terrain on which the call for a Black agenda is being fought. Take, for instance, the question of land and housing construction. While this forms a cornerstone of any policy agenda, and in general terms is something around which all sectors of African-Americans can unite, the practice followed is dramatically different. Although there are no fixed boundaries between positions we can identify three general policy differences: First, a demand for more housing. This is a traditional position, and whether advocated by people on the left or the right, challenges little in the structure of housing creation and allocation. Second, individual entrepreneurialism, specifically giving minority developers a cut of the action. This position is a democratic demand which essentially holds that all forms of discrimination which have eliminated minority developers from participating in the construction market-place be eliminated. Although it is democratic and a position to which progressives should lend some level of support, this demand is a key position of the newer and more aggressive sectors of the Black middle class. While this challenges *who* is responsible for the development, it does not challenge *how* the development takes place. Third, community land trusts and cooperative housing efforts. This position is a developing view among many progressives calling for a collective community approach to land control and development. Essentially this last position demands that land be eased away from private, individual control and that a pattern of leasing be established. Limited equity cooperatives, for example, offer working-class people some of the benefits of ownership, along with a financially feasible means to enter the market-place.

Again, there is no brick wall between these positions. Indeed, the same grouping can find itself advocating in one form or another all three policies. What is important to note, however, is that each of the three positions represents different tendencies for Black agenda forces. Each contains a different vision of structural reform in the capitalist USA.

These differences can also be found in the arena of employment and industrial development. In the face of a declining manufacturing sector and the erosion of the US industrial base there have been several different responses. Of relevance to this discussion is the demand for jobs pure and simple. This demand can be answered, in a peculiar manner, by Reaganite practice. After all, under Reagan, millions of jobs were in fact produced. The problem, however, remains one of the content of these jobs. As noted earlier, service-sector employment has been gaining ground at the expense of manufacturing.

In the demand for jobs there are several different policy options. There is the "take what you can get" line of thought, which is to say little or no strategic planning, and accepting whatever the market makes possible. Create a shopping mall, for instance, regardless of the content of the jobs produced and the needs of the community.

The more ominous policy option is one which surfaced in the early 1980s, then went into relative hibernation, and is only now re-emerging, that is, "enterprise zones." Born out of an approach developed in Britain to deal with their economic crisis, the enterprise zones are essentially versions of Southeast Asia brought to the Western capitalist world. The theory is simple: eliminate as many "obstacles" to business development and the cities (or whatever target) will rise again. The main inducement to industries to return to or enter the enterprise zones are tax breaks (though other incentives are often offered, such as the elimination or reduction of health and safety standards for workers). The particular danger raised by renewed discussions regarding enterprise zones is that they appeal to "common sense," that is, the schematic views held by the masses at any given time influenced by the dominant philosophy of that era and that specific formation, to para-phrase Italian Marxist Antonio Gramsci.[6] "Common sense" says that industry deserted the cities due to government restrictions, high taxes, unions and social legislation. "Common sense" says that industry went to those regions of the US (or offshore) lacking such legislation. Therefore, the conclusion is obvious: provide inducements by eliminating the disincentives.

With the appointment of former New York Congressman Jack Kemp to head the Department of Housing and Urban Development (HUD), support for the enterprise zone concept has gained some ground and not solely among neo-conservatives. The decline in heavy industry and the creation of "employment" via the narcotics trade has every sector of the African-American population looking for answers.

Leaving aside for a moment the reactionary nature of the enterprise zone as a policy option, the scheme has questionable validity even within bourgeois circles. One Baltimore area capitalist speaking of the enterprise zone project in his area noted: "The enterprise zone benefits are so minimal that I haven't concerned myself with them."[7] The General Accounting Office of the US government, commenting on three such zones in Maryland, states that the zones "did not stimulate local economic growth."[8] The GAO found that infrastructure, low crime rates and access to labor markets were more important in attracting business than were tax incentives. This analysis is consistent with other such commentaries which have uniformly noted that tax incentives are rarely sufficient inducements to promote new economic development and investment.

As a policy option the enterprise zone is a thoroughly reactionary concept. In essence it is attempting to promote competition with capitalist industries within the Third World on those terms. In order to do this a massive decline in the standard of living of the US worker along with his/her general conditions of work are necessitated since multi-national capital moves to the Third World seeking lower labor costs and the removal of other such "encumbrances" on the exercise of its influence. For any section of Afro-America to advocate such policies is to promote the further immiseration of the Black working class.

Alternative industrial development strategies are not very popular due largely to the very different premises posed. Yet such approaches are becoming a more recognizable facet of the progressive trend within Afro-America. Industrial cooperative advocate and Boston-based community activist Chuck Turner frames his approach as follows:

perpetuating this idea [that the needs of capital should dominate over the

needs of labor in the context of the community development movemen
subtly undercuts the goal of psychological as well as material empowerment
of the members of the community. If the businesses spawned by the
community development efforts continue their traditions of worker powerlessness, the only substantive change in condition is that the workers are
now dependent on owners of capital who are potentially more responsive
than the traditional capitalist. While this may improve their material
condition, it does nothing to strengthen their ability to shape their reality.[9]

The creation of industrial cooperatives, however, is only one small
piece of the alternative method. The worker cooperative model speaks
to the specific internal dynamics of a business or industry. It does not,
in and of itself, speak to the method of promoting development. In this
sense, the worker cooperative model is not, *ipso facto*, the response to
the enterprise zone strategy.

An interesting approach to the question of economic development
has emerged in Boston Black and Latino communities. The following
will touch on two examples: one is in the discussion stage and the other
is the more fully developed experiment known as the Dudley Street
Neighborhood Initiative. The center of the Roxbury section of Boston
has long been a depressed area. Though Dudley Station in particular
had been a thriving shopping area, over the last twenty years it has
fallen on harder times, particularly with the rise of suburban shopping
malls and a revitalized downtown Boston. When Boston became the
target of massive development (particularly with the increase in finance
and information processing), office space came to be in short supply.
The central area for new office space was Boston's downtown; however, in time the conception of such expansion brought plans for such
development to the doorstep of the Boston Black community.

The South End of Boston, bordering the area around the Prudential
Center and the John Hancock building, became the target of 1970s
development, in this case housing. Condominium conversion became
the watchword as a multi-racial, working-class community became
increasingly yuppified. With new business development came an influx
of new residents and the search for housing. Over the 1980s, housing
and rental costs in Boston sky-rocketed to place it among the top three
US cities in terms of housing expense. As the South End changed,
development moved towards the heart of the Black community.

Coinciding with the increased housing development (which only
later in the game became a focus of attention for a rising Black
development sector) was new discussion about business creation in the
Dudley Station area. This discussion took place in the context of the

removal of the Massachusetts Bay Transportation Authority's (MBTA) elevated railroad system (the "Orange Line") from the Washington St Corridor. This project, which was completed with the creation of a new Orange Line route running closer to the gentrified Jamaica Plain and South End sections of Boston, altered the picture of the Black community. Thus Dudley Station became the focus of attention for new business development schemes, some of which originated in City Hall and the Boston Redevelopment Authority (BRA – a quasi-public agency connected to the City and whose director is appointed by the Mayor of Boston).

The struggle around development and land control took a new and more programmatic form in the mid 1980s with the creation of the Organizing Committee for a Greater Roxbury Neighborhood Authority (GRNA). Influenced from its inception by former state representative and two-time mayoral candidate Mel King, this organization began to act as an alternative pole around which gathered progressive forces in the Black community intent on reducing the loss of land and the expulsion of Black people from Boston.

While the GRNA focused the bulk of its time on matters relating to housing and land development (perhaps most interestingly creating an "eviction free zone" in which efforts were undertaken to reduce housing speculation and wholesale evictions of the neighborhood's indigenous population), a subsection of GRNA began discussions concerning plans which were being floated in many different arenas regarding business development. The thrust of the plans under discussion was that additional office and retail space should be created for Boston by the development of the Dudley Station area.

The response to these plans took about two years to formulate. Drawing from a program sponsored by the Massachusetts Executive Office of Labor, known as the Cooperative Regional Industrial Laboratory (CRIL), the subcommittee of GRNA began to develop a proposal for a committee to oversee and promote industrial development in Boston's Black community. The CRIL was a notion developed in part based on ideas flowing from Britain's now-defunct Greater London Council. The CRIL is a program created to respond to plant closings. As such it not only provides assistance to displaced workers, but also looks at alternative uses for plants which are shut down and, where possible, promotes the introduction of new industries.

The architects of what has come to be known as the Greater Roxbury Industrial Commission (GRIC) used the CRIL as a model, in part as one possible access to funding. The original concept behind the GRIC was that a committee should be established which promoted industrial development in the Black community. Specifically, it was stressed that the proposed introduction of additional office and retail employment would do nothing for the skill level of the workers in the Greater Roxbury area. The thinking also held that the development of light manufacturing would be one means of re-establishing blue-collar employment which would provide a higher income base for the Black and Latino population in the Greater Roxbury area.

The GRIC (at the time of writing) can be said to be in embryo. Through preliminary research, however, it determined that: (a) there is little information about the current workforce in the Greater Roxbury area, specifically information regarding which skills *currently* exist within the community, and (b) that there are light manufacturing firms which are interested in locating in Boston but have not done so primarily because of the lack of properly zoned space and the intense competition with the commercial sector for space.

The orientation of the GRIC, which includes area community activists, trade unionists, agency directors and small business people, is to build an organization which can intervene in current discussions regarding the economic development of Greater Roxbury. Such intervention is aimed at reorienting the type of development which is planned for the area. The GRIC's objective is not simply the promotion of employment, but the promotion of jobs which carry with them liveable wages (and this is one of the distinctions between its view and that of the proponents of enterprise zones). Additionally, it is recognizing the need to build support mechanisms for existing businesses in the Greater Roxbury area (for example, the creation of a clearing-house for information which can assist small businesses in surviving). The GRIC is also seeking a means to promote individual enterprises as well as worker-based cooperatives. One aspect of the latter is seeking a policy by which owners of firms in the Greater Roxbury area will be asked, before they consider closing or moving their firms, to sell their firms to the workers who operate them. The GRIC would then seek out the technical assistance to make such a transfer possible.

As mentioned, the GRIC is at an early stage in development, but it has already run into some opposition, which takes the form of "pragmatic opposition" and "ideological opposition." The pragmatic opposition simply believes that the GRIC 's plans are unrealistic and that whatever jobs come to the community should be accepted. The ideological opponents, one of whom was a former Black elected official, consider the idea of a committee overseeing and promoting a specific type of development wrong on principle. Rather – and here they

dovetail with the pragmatic opponents – they believe public intervention in the development process should be discouraged.

It is around this question of public intervention that the character of
a Black agenda for economic development becomes both critical and
sharp. The founders of the GRIC formulated the notion of such a group
precisely because the economic devastation of the Greater Roxbury
community (as with Black and Latino communities around the USA) is
not simply a problem of the market-place. Largely white firms have
chosen not to invest in Black and Latino communities. And, when such
firms do enter, it is largely in the interest of getting cheaper labor.
Leaving economic development to the genius of the market-place or to
the whims of City Hall will not produce any basic change in the
situation facing the Black and Latino worker. Thus the demands for the
economic development of the Black and Latino communities cannot be
assumed to have a neutral character. The types of enterprises, the
nature of the wages and working conditions and the conditions under
which a business enters the community, all reflect a class viewpoint on
development, and more generally a class viewpoint on how the survival
of the Afro-American is to take place.

Whether the GRIC will succeed is a matter for speculation. The road
which it is promoting should be examined in all matters relating to a
Black agenda. The GRIC, along with the Dudley Street Neighborhood
Initiative, is attempting to chart a different course. Both are promoting
the notion of public intervention and ultimately control over development. Such notions not only put them at odds with the pragmatic and
ideological opponents noted above, but also with a set of Black
developers who embrace the notion of private and individual control
over any and all development. This basic contradiction exists within
and among the forces attempting to promote a Black agenda. The
resolution of it will probably shape the economic future of the Black
worker specifically, and Afro-America generally, for the next several
generations.

The Dudley Street Neighborhood Initiative (DSNI) is the other, more
fully developed representative of an alternative development strategy.
Based in the middle of a diverse ethnic community, the DSNI is a non-
profit planning organization founded in 1984. Area residents, organizations and agencies sought to form an independent, elective body
which would address problems of vacant land, crime, housing and
social service needs. Within one year of its founding money was raised
to hire a minority planning firm which over an eighteen-month period
worked with the people of the neighborhood to design the type of
community which reflected the needs and concerns of residents. A

central feature of this process was the inclusion of popular involvement and the control of land by the residents.

Subsequent to the development of the plan, the DSNI approached the city of Boston to become a "121A" corporation which would allow them, through the power of eminent domain, to seize vacant land. The DSNI succeeded in this effort. In addition to this historic step, the city agreed to give the DSNI access to fifteen acres of public land through a joint planning partnership between the city and the DSNI. The Plan envisions 367 units of new housing, and the rehabbing of 500 existing units. It also calls for developing commercial property, childcare centers, and upgrading human service agencies. Key to this will be strong block associations to keep the community organized. In order to finance the Plan, the DSNI has tapped into public and private sources of funds.

The DSNI differs from the community development corporation model in that the CDC conducts the development work itself. The DSNI, on the other hand, seeks developers who will construct proposals within the framework developed by the organization. The major justification for the DSNI is not development *per se* but rather insuring that development is planned and implemented in ways that allow the residents to control the purposes for which land is used.

The structure of the DSNI was designed to assist in this effort. Elections to the Board of Directors occur every two years. The Board is organized to reflect a composition which includes 60 per cent residents, 20 per cent human service agencies, 10 per cent community development corporations, and 10 per cent for small businesses and churches. In addition to this, the Board has a mandate to reflect the ethnic diversity of the neighborhood; this includes reserved seats on the Board for African-Americans (at least three), Cape Verdeans (at least three), Latinos (at least three), and whites (at least three). Although the DSNI is still experiencing growing pains as a new organization, with a different kind of planning philosophy, it does represent an approach which contrasts with the traditional liberal and neo-conservative approaches for economic development in the Black community. It is an approach which rejects the notion of vouchers, trickle-down dynamics, or free enterprise zones; it is an approach that emphasizes the control of land and development by the people who live on the land, and are most affected by the development decisions that are made.

The two examples discussed briefly here, GRIC and the DSNI, represent concrete examples of alternatives to the traditional models of community and economic development. Both represent a different, more progressive, approach for Black community and economic development. Neither is based on what neo-conservatives might refer to as government handouts; they both rely, instead, on the political mobilization of the residents of an area in order to control the direction of land development. These models also avoid the paternalism inherent in many liberal approaches to the generation of Black social and economic mobility; neither of these approaches questions the intelligence, values, norms or motivation of poor and working-class people. Instead they rely on a progressive vision of utilizing land development in the American city to respond directly to the needs of people in a community; there is an acknowledgment, also, that land development must be tied directly to the well-being of people. And it is the people in a neighborhood who should be entrusted with the political power to ensure that development is pursued in people-oriented ways. These kinds of models will be very important as the calls for Black agendas increase across the nation. Undoubtedly, they will generate debates regarding how African-Americans might effectively pursue economic development. These two models are showing that in some sectors of the Black community there are definite ideas about what the most effective answers are for the Black community and economic development; answers that have not been reflected in the traditional discussions between liberals and neo-conservatives.

Notes

1. Jeff Faux, "The Market-System Problem: The National Context," in Severyn T. Bruyn and James Meehan, *Beyond the Market and the State: New Directions in Community Development* (Philadelphia: Temple University Press, 1987), p. 30.

2. "The False Paradise of a Service Economy," *Business Week*, March 3, 1986, p. 79.

3. "Careers and Opportunities 1989," *Black Enterprise*, February 1989, p. 68.

4. Theodore Cross, *The Black Power Imperative* (New York: Faulkner Publishers, 1984).

5. We are not here trying to blur distinctions. Rather we are attempting to discuss the role which these socio-economic groupings play in the real world. Given African-Americans' status as an oppressed nationality within the USA, the fundamental reality of class has been distorted by a fundamentally racist society. An example of the consequences of this distortion is the periodic camaraderie between the Black bourgeoisie and the Black poor and working class in struggles for Black economic development.

6. *Selections from the Prison Notebooks of Antonio Gramsci*, edited and translated by Quintin Hoare and Geoffrey Nowell Smith (New York: International Publishers, 1971), p. 419.

7. Quoted in Ron Stodghill II, Patrick Cole, Teresa McGuire, "Enterprise Zones – Or Twilight Zones?," *Business Week*, February 27, 1989, p. 113.

8. Ibid., p. 113.

9. Chuck Turner, "Worker Cooperative and Community Development," in Bruyn and Meehan, *Beyond the Market*, pp. 66–7.

The Theory of Vouchers and Housing Availability in the Black Community

Sheila Ards

Billions of dollars are spent each year housing the poor. In 1985 over fourteen billion dollars were spent on housing benefits to low-income individuals.[1] And yet the number of families in the homeless population is on the rise. National estimates of the homeless range from a low of 192,000 to a high of 2.2 million persons.[2] Families comprise 21 per cent of the homeless. The housing problems of the poor seem to be escalating rather than abating. Are the housing programs, which were designed with poor disadvantaged families in mind, fulfilling the policy objectives? Are the billions of dollars which are being spent actually solving the housing problems of the poor, particularly in Black urban communities?

Policy-makers in the past decade hoped to answer these questions affirmatively with the introduction of new and controversial housing programs. One such program is the "Section 8 Housing Voucher Program" which provides direct cash for housing assistance to low-income families. Unlike conventional public housing programs which focus on direct provision of housing, voucher-subsidized rental payments are designed to give families greater variability in housing choice. The voucher, based on a fair market rent (FMR) for housing in the locality and a percentage of family income, is given to an eligible family for the purpose of offsetting housing costs; the actual rent of the housing unit can exceed the FMR. Unlike the other Section 8 programs, the voucher is tied to the family and not the rental unit. A family that qualifies for a voucher is able to move and carry the voucher to a new locational choice. The free mobility with the voucher is thought to encourage greater bargaining between the tenant and landlord, allegedly resulting in better quality housing for the tenant. This assumes, of course, that the availability of housing to all, regardless of race, is in fact an attribute of a "free-market" system. Housing vouchers have been the cornerstone of the Republican national administration housing strategy for the poor over the past nine years and policy analysts have recommended shifting the federal focus from public housing to housing subsidies. This has become a popular call for many economists, including Anthony Downs who recommends the availability of housing vouchers "to all renting households with incomes below 50 percent of the area wide median."[3]

Findings from the first year of the voucher program raise concerns for the Black urban community. Blacks were less likely to receive vouchers compared to their white counterparts and Black success rate in obtaining vouchers was 57 per cent compared to a white success rate of 75 per cent. And, when Blacks received vouchers, they paid more in average rent than whites. Blacks paid an average monthly rent of $467.85 compared to an average monthly rent paid of $426.85 paid by whites.[4] It is possible that the housing solution heralded by many is not the answer for the Black community.

Vouchers are based on the economic principle that increased "consumerization" of housing services ought to generate greater benefits to the users–tenants and landlords. Voucher recipients (tenants), through the rent subsidies, are thought to have greater demand power and buying potential. The demand power should result in better housing quality. The extra buying potential should result in greater housing quantity. The philosophical rationalization for this approach can be found in the ideas and works of conservatives such as Milton Friedman, and more recently, Thomas Sowell.[5] This article examines the theoretical validity of this kind of approach by investigating whether Black families actually receive greater housing demand power and buying potential. Housing subsidies have been praised by both neo-conservatives and liberals. The liberals "recently praised such proposals on the grounds that they provide an efficient means for adjusting the supply of housing to the desires of consumers, that they will increase demand for standard units, and that they permit the consumer more freedom to choose a location and housing style that he likes."[6]

It should be pointed out that housing subsidies are only one of several approaches suggested by neo-conservatives in response to housing problems. Another approach is simply to disperse the poor. Although there are a few well-known Black neo-conservatives expounding this view today perhaps the most prominent scholar of this idea is Edward C. Banfield.[7] Almost two decades ago he argued that problems associated with the poor and Blacks in American cities were not due to racism, "benign neglect," or governmental retrenchment of social commitment, but rather to the attitudes and group culture of the poor and lower-class citizenry. And therefore, he reasoned, the major strategy for dealing with the problems of the poor should focus on physically eliminating people in this category from the American city, instead of helping them directly with their problems. In other words: not better, more professional human services, and greater spending on housing, but smaller numbers of poor people through forced sterilization and physical dispersement. Poverty and the human services crisis, according to this analysis, are simply caused by too many people who are lazy and shiftless. Furthermore, there is an underlying premise in this analysis that it is useless to help the poor because these problems are inherent in their culture.

This approach simply excuses political forces which in turn maintain racism and contextual situations causing and perpetuating the social, educational and employment crisis in the Black community. While voucher programs escape the nefarious tinge of Banfield's proposals, and others such as those of former New York City housing administrator Roger Starr, this approach does not provide an adequate response because it also overlooks racism and other causes of the housing problem facing Blacks. Vouchers should also be viewed with caution for another reason: they do not capitalize on the resources of the Black *community*, instead they respond solely to individuals and families. While one may argue that the collective benefits of individuals will in the long run lead to increased benefits to society, there is the possibility that short-run outcomes may lead to the dissolution and further weakening of the housing stock in the Black community.

There are two questions this paper seeks to answer: (1) Does the utilization of vouchers significantly assist Blacks in need of housing? and (2) Do liberal and conservative assumptions regarding housing and race fail to respond to the needs of Blacks? First a brief history of the housing voucher program is presented. The assumptions regarding race and racial inequality of housing choice are then examined. Next, critiques of the conceptual and programmatic weaknesses of housing vouchers are detailed. And finally alternative housing policy directions for Blacks are discussed.

The housing problems of the poor have perplexed policy-makers for decades. The ideological and political foundation for much of the housing policy of the last fifty or so years can be traced to the New Deal era. The US Housing Act of 1937 sought to provide reduced-rent public housing to low-income families who were unable to provide adequate housing for their family needs. Jeremiah Cotton, in Chapter 1, notes the spillover benefits and obligations of the federal government to intervene in the market economy as it affects the Black community. In a market economy, there are two ways to increase the quantity and quality of housing for the poor. One is through supply-side strategies; and the other is through changing demand. Over the past five decades, both paths have been pursued simultaneously. To increase the quantity of quality housing for the poor (supply-side strategy) the federal government built public housing to warehouse the poor; also, it provided subsidies for the construction of new housing and the rehabilitation of existing housing within the private sector.

Conservative advocates of housing assistance to low-income households have generally supported providing families with housing units as opposed to supplying direct cash transfers. They argue that housing, unlike other household goods, is easily evaluated and measurable; there are standards of safe, clean and decent housing. A housing unit cannot be traded or sold for drugs and unnecessary luxuries. Thus, like food, housing ought to be provided directly to the needy. This view asserts that cash transfers never guarantee that the poor will be fed or housed adequately.[8]

After years of providing public housing in crime-ridden and deteriorating tenant complexes and after coming to the realization that building new houses would not alleviate all of the housing needs of the poor, public officials sought alternative forms of housing assistance to solve this problem.[9] Nathan Glazer noted that "Public housing is a graveyard of good intentions . . . But to turn public housing into sound, low-cost family housing seems enormously difficult."[10] Rental of the existing housing stock was encouraged; thus demand-side strategies were undertaken.

One demand-side strategy is the housing voucher program. One objective of the housing voucher program is to provide individuals with greater choice of housing to meet their individual housing needs.[11] In effect, the housing voucher increases the family income available to purchase a bundle of goods. It does not increase the stock of available and decent housing. Nor does it allow for control over the cost of housing. Technically speaking, vouchers do not respond to the housing needs of Black *communities*, but rather to the need for individuals and families to find available housing, whether in the Black or another community.

The Black community has been shown to have the highest percentage of dilapidated housing units. Non-white households are more likely to live in crowded units lacking adequate plumbing than white households. Vouchers do nothing to increase the adequacy of housing units in the Black community. The potential receipt of vouchers requires the family either to move from squalid conditions or to induce bargaining between the tenant and the landlord. Landlords within the Black community are faced with either improving the housing unit conditions or allowing the voucher tenant to move. Given the high demand for housing within the Black community, the landlord will more than likely decide not to improve the housing unit but to rent to a non-voucher tenant, forcing the voucher recipient to move to a new locational choice.

This scenario is consistent with results from the *First Year Findings*. The results showed that 75.3 per cent of Blacks had to move to find a housing unit that met the housing standards of the local housing authority. Only 48 per cent of whites had to move. Given the inadequate quantity of housing units which meet local public housing authority standards, some Blacks must move out of predominantly Black communities and are forced to pay much higher rents.

Housing vouchers were designed to encourage low-income families to actively seek better housing but they have not encouraged those families to invest or to build or control housing in their own communities.[12] Theoretically, the voucher recipient has control over where he will live and the amount he will expend on housing to the extent that vouchers are accepted by the landlord. Two studies, conducted during the 1970s, played a major role in the present design of the Section 8 Housing Voucher program. One was the Experimental Housing Allowance Program (EHAP); the second study evaluated the New Construction and Existing Housing components of the Section 8 Housing Assistance payment program. Both studies provided insights about the potential of subsidies to improve housing prospects for the poor.

Some of the findings from the EHAP experiments suggested that the expectations associated with vouchers were not well founded. Not only were participation rates much lower under the voucher program than under other income transfer programs, but most of the allowance payment was spent on non-housing items. The only encouraging benefit was that rent burdens under vouchers decreased from 40 to 25 per cent.[13]

Housing vouchers were also thought to be potential tools of advancing the racial integration of neighborhoods. Once a family had the resources to choose a housing location, the family would live in the neighborhood with better facilities. The neighborhoods which in the past have been linked to better facilities have been neighborhoods that were predominantly white.[14]

The EHAP experiment showed that housing subsidies did not result in the level of integration that some policy analysts had suggested – or perhaps feared. The results from the experiments showed very little spatial rearrangement between neighborhoods. Although there was some movement out of low-income neighborhoods into integrated neighborhoods and from there to white neighborhoods, these flows were insignificant in altering housing-market conditions in either the sending or receiving neighborhoods.[15] Although the EHAP experiment did not show the dissolution of the Black community, the vitalization of Black communities and the strengthening of a Black housing base were not policy goals.

So with the "free" market and increased resources for purchasing housing goods and increased demand for housing quality, why do we still see all-white and all-Black neighborhoods? Neither liberal nor conservative economists have responded adequately to this, given their faith in vouchers and the free market. Conservative economists have argued that race plays little role in a landlord's decision to rent to a tenant. The major factors are money and profits. If a tenant has the resources to rent a unit, then the profit-maximizing landlord would be irrational not to rent to the tenant.

There are several theoretical and conceptual weaknesses associated with vouchers. One is that there is no such thing as a free market when it comes to housing and race. As several major studies have pointed out since the publication of the Kerner Commission, America remains a segregated society.[16] There exists in this society a racial hierarchy that keeps Black and white sectors economically, educationally and residentially segmented from each other. If this is accurate, then the claim of a free market is unfounded and policies assuming the existence of such a market are doomed to fail.

Another weakness of the idea of voucherization in housing is the implicit suggestion that Blacks should leave Black communities in order to find decent and available housing. This weakens vouchers as a viable solution to the needs of Black families for housing. The New Construction experiment showed that Blacks were unwilling to leave their network of family and friends in search of housing that met the housing standards for the voucher receipt. Furthermore, voucherization, as it was presented by policy-makers, put no emphasis on improving the housing stock within Black communities, and in encouraging Black control over this same housing stock. Vouchers seem to reflect the calls for the dispersal of the Black community that came from liberal circles in the aftermath of the urban riots in the sixties. Vouchers bypass the possibility of developing housing within the Black community as a response to the housing needs of individual Blacks.

There are also two major programmatic weaknesses of the housing voucher program. One is the small quantity of quality housing; and the other is the lack of control over housing cost. There is a relatively small quantity of quality housing units which accept vouchers. Conservatives would argue that voucher recipients would have greater choice of available housing units; they argue that vouchers present the least constraints within the housing market, and this in turn should produce greater housing choice. But due to the small quantity of units available, choice for the recipient may be limited rather than expanded.

There is another problem with some of the assumptions tied to vouchers and housing for poor persons – the control over cost. Decision theory can be used to show why a landlord would seek higher rents from voucher tenants. We can categorize the landlord's decision process as risk neutral, risk taking, or risk averse. A risk neutral situation is when the landlord is assured of the rent whether the tenant has a voucher or not. Then the landlord is indifferent to who becomes the tenant. A risk-taking situation is when the prior probability of receiving the rent from a voucher recipient is lower than the prior probability of receiving rent from a tenant who doesn't have a voucher. In an area where the demand for quality housing is high, the landlord is able to find a tenant who has the ability to pay the entire rental cost. For the landlord to choose a tenant whose probability of being able to pay is lower, he must increase the rental cost to that tenant to justify the lower probability of receiving the rent. This would result in higher rents to a voucher recipient for the same quality of housing than a person without a voucher would pay. This of course is contrary to the theoretical objective of vouchers. This argument is not new but merely a descriptive formulation of Sowell's explanation of higher rents to recipients of housing subsidies. A risk averse landlord is skeptical about renting the unit to a tenant whose probability of paying the rent is substantially less than one. Therefore, profit may dictate to the landlord that he or she not rent a unit to a voucher recipient if the rental cost is greater than the fair market rate.

The introduction of race may further increase the cost of housing to Black recipients. Black voucher recipients are shown to pay 10 per cent more in gross rents than their white counterparts participating in the voucher program. Thus Black voucher recipients face two penalties: the first is being a voucher recipient; the second is being Black.

Presently large numbers of voucher recipients are unable to find housing units. Recipients with vouchers are staying in crowded conditions with friends, relatives, or in shelters for homeless families. This situation seems totally contradictory to a profit-maximizing situation. Traditional economics would suggest that more landlords would step in and offer housing units at varying rents, until the rental price reaches the fair market rent or until profits reach zero. But why haven't more landlords offered to participate in the housing voucher market?

One reason could be reluctance to become entangled in governmental bureaucracy. Another is that the government's guaranteed participation in the housing voucher program is for a short period of time; thus, the landlord doesn't want to be stuck with an ex-voucher recipient who cannot pay the rent. Or third, landlords would prefer a rent subsidy that is guaranteed whether or not the tenant pays. We cannot overlook, furthermore, the historical role that white landlords have played in maintaining residential segregation. Why should one assume that the racial hierarchy that so many have spoken about, and the maintenance of rigid racial residential segregation that has been voluminously documented in government and scholarly reports, would all of a sudden be overcome as a consequence of vouchers? As a basically administrative mechanism, the voucherization of housing services cannot reverse the historical and social roles of white landlords in protecting white urban and suburban turf from potential Black residents except when such areas are undergoing some kind of social or cultural transition.

Over the past five decades both conservative and liberal policymakers have failed to provide effective ideas and policy suggestions for adequate housing for the lower-income Black segment of society. Vouchers have not been the appropriate answer for the Black community. Then what should be done in this area? Our entire policy for how we "help" low-income and moderate families in Black communities should be reconsidered. Since the New Deal lower-income groups have been treated as if they were incapable of making financial decisions about the allocation of money towards food and shelter.

Public policies in the area of human services and housing, especially as implemented in Black urban communities, have not incorporated the lower-income individuals into every facet of decision-making which affects their lives. This must change, because housing for the Black community will not be improved or expanded until Blacks can politically control decisions which affect the housing stock in these communities. Voucherization seeks to respond to the needs of individual consumers, not to community-wide needs. Blacks must become more politically aggressive in determining what are the community-wide needs in the area of housing and seek systemic remedies, not those based on conceptualizing the Black community as a mere conglomeration of individuals or consumers. These views are not so different from those expressed by Cloward and Piven in their classic work, *Regulating the Poor*.[17]

Certain policies, like direct cash subsidies to individuals, or wage policies ensuring decent levels of buying power for families, may work better than vouchers. But the idea of improving the access of Blacks to decent and affordable housing, separated from policies and programs that improve the housing stock already available in Black communities, as well as the control of this housing stock by its residents, will fail. What this means is that Blacks cannot turn to more government, as the neo-conservatives contend, to meet their housing needs. Many governmental programs emerging out of the New Deal and Great Society bypass the Black community and seek to respond only to the Black individual or the Black family. But the neo-conservative claims regarding the advantages of a free market are also a weak response to the housing needs of Blacks. Rather than engaging in a debate that will not improve substantively the quality of housing for the Black community, Black leadership should instead use available governmental resources to invest in housing that will respond to community-wide needs, and in mobilizing politically residents to begin controlling the land which they occupy. This theme is repeated in other chapters in this book, including those by Walter Stafford, William Fletcher and Eugene Newport. This would be the most effective approach to the housing needs of Black communities in urban America.

Notes

1. *Statistical Abstract of the United States: 1988* (108th edn) (Washington, DC: US Bureau of the Census, 1987).

2. Kathleen Proch and Meslin A. Taber, "Helping the Homeless," *Public Welfare* (Spring 1987), pp. 5–9.

3. Anthony Downs, *Rental Housing in the 1980s* (Washington, DC: The Brookings Institute, 1983), p. 144.

4. Stephen D. Kennedy and Merly Finkel, "Report of First Year Findings for the Freestanding Housing Voucher Demonstration" (Cambridge, MA: Abt Associates, Inc., June 26, 1987).

5. See Milton Friedman, *Capitalism and Freedom* (Chicago: University of Chicago Press, 1982) and Thomas Sowell, *Markets and Minorities* (New York: Basic Books, 1981).

6. Irving Welfeld, "Toward a New Federal Housing Policy," *The Public Interest*, no. 19 (Spring 1970), pp. 31–43.

7. Edward Banfield, *The Unheavenly City Revisited* (Boston: Little, Brown and Co., 1974)

8. Welfeld, "Toward a New Federal Housing Policy."

9. Ibid., pp. 31–43.

10. Nathan Glazer, "Housing Problems and Housing Policy," *Public Interest*, no. 7 (Spring 1967), pp. 21–51.

11. Kennedy and Finkel, "First Year Findings."

12. Claire Hammond, *The Benefits of Subsidized Housing Programs: An Intertemporal Approach* (Cambridge, UK: Cambridge University Press, 1987).

13. Ira S. Lowry, *Experimenting with Housing Allowances: The Final Report of the Housing Assistance Supply Experiment* (Cambridge, Mass.: Oelgeschlager, Gunn & Hain, Publishers, 1983).

14. Ibid.

15. Ibid.

16. John M. Goering, "Minority Housing Needs and Civil Rights Enforcement," in Jamshid Momeni, ed., *Race, Ethnicity and Minority Housing in the United States* (Westport, Conn.: Greenwood Press, 1986), pp. 195–216.

17. Richard A. Cloward and Francis Fox Piven, *Regulating the Poor: The Functions of Public Welfare* (New York: Vintage Books, 1971).

9

The Colonizing Impact of Public Service Bureaucracies in Black Communities

Jacqueline Pope

Black America's social and economic fabric cannot be fully understood or analyzed without reference to a context of complex and oppressive public assistance bureaucratization. The current bureaucratization of public assistance pervades many aspects of social and economic life in the Black community. Expanding communities composed primarily of African-Americans are a significant problem for a society that espouses democratic ideals in that these concentrations are characterized by large tracts of poverty, and social alienation. In this context the most oppressive tendencies of those public and private interests aligned with the political, economic and cultural status quo are most evident in low-income African-American communities.

Public service bureaucracies, as pointed out by urban scholars C.V. Hamilton, Francis Fox Piven and Richard Cloward, and, in this volume, James Jennings and Mack Jones, are critical tools in the network of institutions that dampen the political empowerment and enlightenment of certain sectors of the African-American population in urban America.[1] It is for this reason that any strategy for the social progress of economically deprived African-American communities must include popular processes for controlling public service bureaucracies, particularly those responsible for the distribution of public assistance. What is referred to here as "bureaucratization" is intensifying and steadily destroying the capacity of African-Americans to develop strategies of empowerment and self-help. Vast numbers of African-Americans are controlled by four major public institutions: the police forces, schools, health agencies and public assistance. Inadvertently or intentionally – in terms of political and social effects it may not matter – these public institutions maintain a watchful eye on the political and cultural activities of African-Americans. These bureaucracies are responsible for blocking and defusing any restlessness or activities that might point towards Black cultural reawakening, self-help, or political empowerment.

This opening statement should not be read as an endorsement of "neo-conservatives" who argue for a free market via corporate tax giveaways, vouchers and privatization, in the delivery of public services such as public assistance, education and housing. Their arguments represent yet another extreme that will continue to keep African-American communities in a subordinate economic, political and cultural position in American society. This opening statement is not a call for the business sector, rather than the public assistance bureaucracies, to do whatever they wish in order to realize profits, and then hope that some of this will trickle down to poor and working-class people in African-American communities. In fact, the development of "free enterprise zones" will fail to improve the economic status of Black communities, as would the increasing power and influence of those public agencies administering social services, because neither approach emphasizes significant political control over public assistance efforts by the populace being affected. The intent of this essay is to raise questions regarding how public service bureaucracies inhibit the political and cultural empowerment of the African-American community; it is presumed here that the acquisition and holding of power is crucial for social and economic advancement.

Bureaucratization of public assistance has meant that poor people are responded to, not as citizens or clients, but as mere recipients. There are major differences in the political behavior of clients, as contrasted to recipients of public services. C.V. Hamilton points out,

> Not only is the patron–recipient relationship depoliticizing in the sense of not making sustained electoral mobilization necessary for the receipt of benefits . . . It might also have the effect of encouraging privatized, individualized responses to problems. A recipient (unlike a client-voter) does not receive benefits as a function of concerted action with others.[2]

This in turn leads to greater difficulties in even conceptualizing grassroots control and impact on the public assistance bureaucracy decision-making. The political control of public assistance agencies is difficult to grasp as a concept; but the administration of public assistance cannot be approached as a technocratic and politically neutral process. Public

assistance agencies rank as the most repressive of political and economic development in African-American communities.

The way public assistance is administered has the effect of depoliti-
cizing large sectors of the African-American urban community.
Moreover, the principal consequence of this process is the dehumaniza-
tion of poor people. Another result is the cultural castration that is
reflected in the policies of public assistance and social services in the
African-American community. Agencies administering public assistance
in African-American communities do not at all seek to educate African-
American people, and to raise their cultural and social consciousness.
This proposal is supported by the work of Piven and Cloward who
have stated, "The bureaucracies therefore manipulate the benefits and
services on which clients come to depend in such a way as to control
their behavior. In this way, governmental benefit systems have become
a powerful source of control over low-income people . . ."[3]

Public assistance can grind away all semblances of dignity and self-
worth, leaving its recipients to hate themselves and conclude, albeit
falsely, that they have no alternatives to provide for themselves and
their children. This has significant implications for the politics of
African-American communities, and the strategies and concepts
necessary in order for these communities to develop socially and
economically.

Today one sees a picture of increasing joblessness and drug use in
some sectors of African-American communities. How do agencies
administering public assistance respond to this kind of situation? Their
apologists provide an inadequate level of services and resources – just
enough to keep people only slightly above a level of abject poverty and
starvation. The institutional posture of public assistance bureaucracies
in African-American communities suggests very clearly that they perceive recipients as worthless and useless.

Unemployment and increasing drug use represent a degree of social
devastation that precludes African-American men from being socially
and economically productive, and therefore marriage and family falter
as critical institutions in the African-American community. And when
the products of this cycle seek public assistance they are basically
castigated and degraded. Recipients of AFDC – and their children – are
viewed as lazy and unproductive. Families on public assistance are
allocated just enough to ward off starvation and homelessness. This
does not leave any time to consider entrepreneurial activities in either
the political or economic arena. Every once in a while politicians,
whether liberal or conservative, Democratic or Republican, come
along with a program to get people off welfare. One typical proposal

calls for the training of recipients so that they may become acceptable as cheap labor. The calls for such training programs have been episodic over the last quarter of a century in the US, but have never been associated with any specific policy strategies that could reduce welfare rolls.

In 1989 one high official in the Department of Employment and Training in Massachusetts, a state whose training programs have received national attention, bragged publicly at a statewide conference on vocational education that through the ET programs thousands of welfare recipients were placed in "quality jobs." But upon being asked what is a "quality job," this bureaucrat replied that this was a job that pays an average of $12,000 per year. This provides a good example illustrating the importance of the recipients to define for themselves "program effectiveness." By controlling the definition of agency "success" or what is considered a "quality" job the recipients of public assistance can hold accountable public service career bureaucrats.

A process of maintaining the sub-dominant status of many African-Americans is also carried out by socialization of the children of mothers on public assistance. How do AFDC children perceive the treatment of their elders and parents by public assistance agencies? Seeing their mothers' degradation at social service offices instills fear, anger and callousness at a very young age. Is it any wonder they may unconsciously opt to reject parental guidance from someone lacking respect and deference from other adults in positions of perceived authority? And as much as we may decry it, is it not logical that some children living in African-American communities will turn to the streets for the affirmation of their humanity and intelligence?

An important element in developing strategies of economic improvement in African-American communities is a populist control of public assistance bureaucracies. This means that the management of public assistance and the public policies circumscribing this management must be democratic, controlled by the people, and for the people. The introduction of political democracy in the management of public assistance will guarantee economic democracy, and this will mean, perhaps, that public assistance resources will be directed towards the elimination of poverty rather than the careers of cold bureaucrats. Democracy, while decried as inefficient by technocrats, offers the possibility of active popular participation and competition among various interest groups.

The bureaucratic organization of public assistance removes all need for face-to-face interaction, providing only the semblance of equality and efficiency. In fact, this perpetuates the agenda and interests of elites and the values that underpin their positions in the social structure. Organizing public assistance with excessive administration guarantees resistance to innovation that might lead to greater efficiency and effectiveness in responding to the needs of the citizenry. The result of excessive bureaucratization in the area of public assistance is limited accountability, incrementalism, turfism, repetition and specialization. These characteristics shield the bureaucracy and its technocrats from the consequences of their decisions. The major political purpose of public assistance bureaucracy becomes, therefore, the acquisition and protection of bureaucratic influence and organizational imperialism. This is quite functional for the maintenance of the social, political and racial status quo.

Public assistance can oppress a community by routinizing services to a point of suffocating collective will and community culture. Completing forms, assigning numbers to human beings, checking applications – all are simple, repetitive and routine chores that impact significantly on the lives of poor people in African-American communities. Moreover, clients can view their lives as marginal, unimportant and hopeless as a result of their treatment in the hands of public servants. Such routinization and minimizing of the social consequences of this relieves the technocrat and the bureaucracy of sympathy and creative thinking. Essentially the system of paper pushers, in and out box stuffers, paperclip counters, janitors, keepers of official stamps, meetings arrangers and so forth, all add up to a system that strips public assistance recipients of their sense of dignity and self-worth. Invariably, if recipients do begin to exert a collective will, expressed periodically in attempts at community control and political accountability, the public assistance bureaucracy calls its handmaiden, "law and order," for help. This means that attempts to reverse a socialization with negative consequences for the public assistance recipient, and the children of such, is resisted fiercely by the public assistance bureaucracy.

What can African-American communities do to begin to control public assistance bureaucracies that determine their social and economic fate? This is a most important organizational and strategic question when it is understood that powerful bureaucracies are just that – *powerful*. The absence of a specific form or proper official stamp or signature on an application can lead to a loss of life-sustaining necessities. How are African-Americans to gain political and consequently perhaps even economic control over public assistance bureaucracies given this reality? Present structures for the delivery of public assistance and human services are destroying or at least discouraging the popular and collective will of African-Americans. This community must now begin to develop alternative ways of dealing with increasing social crisis. This challenge becomes especially important given the exodus of upwardly mobile African-Americans from the poorer and working-class residential areas.

One successful model for challenging public bureaucracies on the part of poor women is offered in the history of the Brooklyn Welfare Action Council.[4] This was a grassroots cooperative started in 1967 and disbanded in 1973. Its purpose was to obtain social and economic benefits for its members through the promotion of changes within the system. The Brooklyn Council distinguished itself by utilizing strategies that empowered its members. It did this by showing its members that only power can be used to confront "the system." But grassroots power had to be based on a community, rather than individual, agenda. The Brooklyn Council organized demonstrations at welfare centers and disruptions at major stores, to show the linkage between the oppression of public service bureaucracies and those interests holding economic power. Although this organization was shortlived, it was effective in giving its members a sense of hope, based on understanding how power operates in the American city.

The idea of "community control," which was reflected in organizations like the Brooklyn Council, must be revived; a new wave of grassroots political mobilization must occur in order for community control to again be considered legitimate and valid. Public sector institutions operating in African-American communities must be forced politically to operate in ways that are not inimical to the economic, educational and cultural interests of African-Americans. Decision-making on the part of the part of public service bureaucracies must be broadened within a democratic context; this means that decision-making processes must institutionalize the presence of both African-Americans living in their own communities and African-American interests.

But while institutional and political accountability of public assistance bureaucracies are vital factors in any scheme for community-based economic development, there must also be a cultural renaissance in the African-American community. Such a cultural and educational renaissance will facilitate political and economic strategies of community development. The public schools, also subject to community control strategies, must be approached as important partners in raising the cultural consciousness of their students, and the parents of their students.

Unless strategies of political and cultural empowerment for African-Americans are pursued, many of the social, economic and educational crises facing this community will not be resolved within the current governmental and policy framework. The problem of increasing drug use and drug-related crime in African-American communities, for example, cannot be solved by the agencies providing public assistance. In fact, in terms of current practices and goals, these agencies are contributors to these kinds of problems. These agencies and their technocratic leaders lack the will, the know-how and an adequate level of resources to control the growing supply of drugs in the African-American community.

As this problem intensifies the response of both liberal and neo-conservative policy advocates is, simply, more law enforcement and more prisons; now we even hear calls for the suspension of constitutional rights in African-American communities plagued by drugs in places like Boston, New York and Washington, DC. These approaches will not work; they are only proposed in order to placate and anesthetize the concerns of the general public. The drug problem in these communities can only be resolved when the demand for drugs is eliminated; but this cannot happen while a people do not understand their worth and importance. The denial of this understanding is perpetuated every day through the interaction between African-Americans and public assistance bureaucracies. Inherent in this is a process of socialization that can be broken only through a program of cultural and racial consciousness. Both experience and the literature on drug abuse prevention have suggested a solution. But, alas, this "solution" may not get a fair hearing in the corridors of policy-makers and by those in positions of being able to have an impact on the reduction of drug-related crimes, especially among African-American and Latino youth.

There is a direct correlation between racial and community consciousness, the level of political influence that a community enjoys, and drug abuse. To inculcate African-American youth with racial consciousness, that is, an understanding and pride in the African-American experience in America, and in the role that African-American youth have played historically in democratizing and modernizing this society, is a sure way of discouraging these same youth from entering the hard drug culture and its violence and disrespect for human life in the communities in which they live. On the basis of experience, we need but to turn to statements contained in the *Autobiography of Malcolm X*, or Claude Brown's *Manchild in the Promised Land*, or even Piri Thomas's *Down These Mean Streets*.[5]

These works illustrate that racial and community consciousness can have – and has had – a positive impact in terms of reducing the problem of drug abuse and related violence in African-American and Latino communities. In his autobiography Malcolm X tells us explicitly how his intellectual growth and understanding of the African-American experience in America led him away from a life of pimping and drug-pushing in the African-American community. What this means is that the cities of America, especially its school systems, must be ready and willing to educate African-American and Latino youth about their culture and race, and about the important contributions that African-Americans and Latinos have made to American society. There is no reason why this should not be part of any public assistance delivery system as well.

But communities also need to have some control over the processes of political economy that determine the amount and flow of drugs into a community. The banks operating in African-American communities, for instance, must either desire or be forced to work cooperatively with the leadership of that community in order to eliminate practices that make the laundering of drug money relatively easy; and the police forces must also respect the African-American community in which they operate. The police leadership must not operate in wanton disre-gard of the well-being of the African-American community, or see the youth of this community as individuals who must continually be put in their place. Are public assistance agencies ready and willing to substi-tute the problem of drug abuse and related violence with racially and culturally sensitive programs for African-American and Latino youth? This is a critical political issue. If the leadership of public assistance agencies were willing to develop strategies to educate African-Ameri-can and Latino youth regarding their culture and the contributions their leaders have made in making America, the problem of drugs and related violence would be solved. Experience and analytical literature tell us this; but, again, is this society ready to deal with masses of African-American and Latino youth who understand their history, and culture – and the political implications of this? Are we ready to deal with an African-American and Latino youth who are articulate about the injustices and inequalities of American society? In responding effectively to the problem of drug abuse and violence in African-American and Latino communities, racial and cultural consciousness must be a critical component. But this will not occur given the current institutional networks that engulf the provision of public assistance in African-American communities. The public service bureaucracies must be forced politically to respond to a progressive agenda of African-American communities.

Since one-third of African-American communities are directly or indirectly affected by public assistance, this must be an important front in developing effective strategies for African-American empowerment. African-American political activists and leaders must again begin to determine and debate how to hold more accountable the public assistance bureaucracies that administer services in our communities; then, they must begin to help mold the professional agenda of these bureaucracies. And on this agenda must be at least two items as suggested in this essay: first, the refusal to degrade the experiences of African-American life in the American city; and secondly, determining how African-Americans can begin to take public dollars and invest them in ways that not only respond to the social and economic needs of their community, but also allow political and community control over such resources.

Notes

1. See Charles V. Hamilton, "Patron Client and Patron Recipient Relations in New York City," *Political Science Quarterly*, vol. 94, no. 2 (Summer 1979); and Francis Fox Piven and Richard A. Cloward, *Regulating the Poor: The Functions of Public Welfare* (New York: Vintage Books, 1971).

2. Hamilton, "Patron Client," p. 225.

3. Richard A. Cloward and Francis Fox Piven, *The Politics of Turmoil: Poverty, Race and the Urban Crisis* (New York: Vintage Books, 1974), p. 8.

4. See Jacqueline Pope, *Biting the Hand That Feeds Them* (Praeger: New York, 1989), and "Women in the Welfare Rights Struggle: The Brooklyn Welfare Action Council" in Juida West and Rhoda Lois Blumberg, eds, *Women and Social Protest* (New York: Oxford University Press, 1990).

5. *The Autobiography of Malcolm X* (New York: Grove Press, 1965); Claude Brown, *Manchild in the Promised Land* (New York: Macmillan, 1965); and Piri Thomas, *Down These Mean Streets* (New York: Knopf, 1967).

10

Understanding the Persisting Crisis of Black Youth Unemployment

Keith Jennings

Youth unemployment in the United States has received an increasing amount of attention over the past few years. The issue has even led the Lutheran Council and other church groups to state that the 1980s may well be remembered for spawning a "lost generation of workers."[1] Youth unemployment has also prompted federal legislative initiatives by a few Congress members, and civic action from several labor unions and social justice agencies. But the situation has continued to worsen.

Massive youth unemployment, especially among African-Americans, when juxtaposed with a conservative federal policy that is more concerned with "Star Wars," budget deficits and school prayer than with meeting human needs, has not allowed the problem to be clearly addressed. Also, the Reagan and Bush administrations and their right-wing backers have propagated the view that racism is no longer an obstacle to Black progress. Instead, they assert that personal inadequacies are the barriers since jobs are available for everyone who "wants to work" and is willing to accept the prevailing wage. Additionally, the best thing the government can do, they say, is to get out of the way and let the "invisible hand" of the market take its course.[2] According to the National Urban League's 1986 State of Black America report, Black teenagers have suffered the sharpest increase in unemployment since 1960, considering all component groups in both the Black and white populations.[3] Real unemployment rates of 58.1 per cent establish Black youth unemployment as one of the most gripping social consequences of the present capitalist economic crisis.

Unemployment is one of the major social ills of a capitalist society. Historically, unemployment (especially among national minority groups) has acted as a social gauge of the growing contradictions within certain societies. Unemployment in Western countries is a visible consequence of the most pronounced economic crisis since the depression of the 1930s. During the first three years of the 1980s the crisis caused a 75 per cent increase in the total number of unemployed persons, an increase from approximately 20 million to 34 million.[4]

The capitalist crisis in the United States is most apparent. The crisis is loosely defined as "frictional unemployment," that is, a temporary situation where workers move from one industry to another in a changing economy. Moreover, when an anti-crisis policy is propagated as "non-inflationary growth" of a new recovery period – normally based on manipulative data – a correct characterization of the crisis is elusive.

The 1970s and the early 1980s have been periods of protracted and stagnated "growth" in the US economy and, by extension, those of the entire capitalist world. The periodic crises of overproduction associated with the business cycles endemic to capitalist economies have been occurring on a more regular basis. Within a five-year period the US economy suffered from two such crises: 1973–75 and 1979–82. In both cases the decline in industrial production was the greatest since the Great Depression. During the 1973–75 and 1979–82 periods US productivity operated at a declining level compared to other nations in Western Europe and Japan, whose infrastructures are newer – hence, their ability to produce higher quality goods at a lower cost is facilitated by new factories and better production techniques. During the two recessions in the US general economic sluggishness did not disappear, not even in the pauses between the crises. For African-Americans, who never really recovered from the first recession, the overall effects have been devastating. Victories scored by national liberation movements in the Third World and the progress made by socialist countries also contributed to the overall economic crisis. These historic developments helped to significantly reduce the share of the world market exploited and controlled by multinational corporations.

Additionally, the drop in the overall rate of labor productivity and industrial growth linked the cyclical disorder with the more protracted structural crisis. The structural crisis hit hardest in the steel, auto, construction, manufacturing and other traditional sectors employing the bulk of semi-skilled and skilled labor.[5] The industrial decline was exacerbated by stagflation, simultaneous high inflation and high unemployment. This occurrence cannot be explained by conventional economic theory. As federal policies were implemented to sustain employment and to ease social contradictions, the multinational corporations (MNCs) ignored the "prescribed recipes." Instead, the

MNCs closed down factories, laid off workers and then moved their operations.[6]

It was at this point that Reagan and his supply-siders entered. Their economic logic read as follows: Lower T . . . leads to increased I. . . E . . . Y . . . C . . . I*. Reagan and his supply-siders believed that a cut in taxes (T) for corporations would encourage them to invest. The investments (I), they argued, would allow corporations to expand, thereby stimulating employment (E). As employment increased, incomes (Y) and consumption (C) would also increase. The larger amount of consumption invariably would produce the incentive for business to invest more (I*) and the economy would continue to expand. The above seems logical, but the fact is that capitalism does not follow logic; it seeks ever-increasing profits.

Since taxes were to "trigger" the supply-siders' equation, taxes were cut and in many instances they were eliminated. In fact fifty of the largest corporations, collectively, paid taxes of less than one per cent over the past five years (1980–85).[7] Moreover, MNCs did not reinvest, upgrade their infrastructures or retain workers, leaving the government unable to abate the problem. Many MNCs moved to the Sun Belt or overseas where they enjoy extended tax holidays and pay lower wages. At the same time, taxes were being cut for the rich and defense spending was increased to record levels. A new arms race was unleashed to the tune of nearly $2 billion – a 75 per cent increase between 1980 and 1984.[8] This, when coupled with high interest rates (deliberately imposed by the Reagan administration to keep inflation down) and high unemployment, forced the national debt to soar to record levels. While Reagan's handling of the crisis represented the right-wing response, it also marked a sharp departure from bourgeois reformist policies.

Noted economist Barry Bluestone points out that unemployment, inflation and falling incomes are indeed complex issues. In analyzing data on deindustrialization and plant closings, Bluestone challenges conventional notions that unemployment is exaggerated or simply frictional: "Workers are not being freed from lower-productivity, lower-wage jobs for work in high-productivity, higher-wage jobs. The opposite is occurring. Workers are skidding downward in the occupational spectrum, not moving up to better jobs and a higher standard of living. The 'high tech' revolution is a case in point."[9]

The Black working class has borne the brunt of this downward economic and social skidding. A number of factors are symptomatic of the crisis:

- After adjusting for inflation, the median cash income of Black families did not change between 1980 and 1984. However, the income gap between Black and white families increased from 56 per cent to 58 per cent during the same period, matching the 1960 level.
- The number of African-Americans living below the poverty level rose from 8.6 million in 1980 to 9.5 million in 1984, or one out of every three.
- Blacks are three times as likely as whites to live in poverty. The Black poverty rate is 33.8 per cent, and 11.5 per cent for whites.
- Fifty-one per cent of Black children live in poverty.
- Despite popular perceptions, increases in the number of female-headed households account for little of the larger increase in poverty since the late 1970s.
- Almost half of all persons living in families headed by a Black woman live in poverty.
- In the last eight years the overall number of families headed by women increased by 700,000 and so did the number of Black males unemployed or out of the labor-force.
- Programs targeted to low-income families and individuals – one-tenth of the federal budget – bore nearly one-third of the 1981–83 budget cuts.
- Seventy-five per cent of all unemployed workers did not receive unemployment benefits in October 1985.

Manning Marable argues that the Black working class has been pre-empted from sections of the capitalist economy targeted for growth in the next decade. He maintains that many African-American workers are occupying white- and blue-collar positions that will no longer be needed in the future.[10] Marable asserts that

> The acceleration of Black unemployment and underemployment, the capitulation of many civil rights and Black power leaders to the right, the demise of militant Black working-class institutions and caucuses, and the growing dependency of broad segments of the Black community upon public assistance programs and transfer payments of various kinds; these interdependent realities within the contemporary Black political economy are the beginning of a new and profound crisis for black labor in America.[11]

Historically the youth unemployment rate has been twice the overall adult rate, but the Black youth unemployment rate has been twice the youth unemployment rates. Congressman John Conyers refers to this as the "two times rule." When viewed beside white youth unemployment

(16.6 per cent), Black youth joblessness (58.1 per cent) is three times as high (unemployment statistics, June 1986).

The following overview provides a picture of joblessness and related issues besetting Black youth:

- Nearly 38 per cent of the more than 8.4 million American unemployed in June 1986 were under twenty-five.
- Between 1979 and 1985 the teenage population declined by almost 13 per cent; however the number of employed teens fell by more than 20 per cent.
- While over 10 million jobs have been created since November 1982, teenagers – representing 18 per cent of the unemployed – have suffered a net job loss of 22,000 jobs and received only one per cent of all jobs.
- The unemployment rate for white teens fell from 16.2 to 14.5 per cent in March 1986, but rose to 16.2 again in June 1986; the Black teen rate rose from 39.1 per cent to 43.7 per cent in March, later to decrease to 40.2 per cent in June 1986.
- Only 26.7 per cent of black teenagers are employed.
- The unemployment rate for 16- to 24-year-old Black high school graduates is 27.3 per cent. This exceeds that of white high school dropouts (23.9 per cent).
- Black college graduates under twenty-five have an unemployment rate of 17.2 per cent in contrast to 4.8 per cent for their white counterparts.
- Only 36.4 per cent of Black high school graduates entered colleges, a substantial decline from 43 per cent in 1980 and 1981.
- Approximately 23.2 per cent of Blacks between the ages of twenty and twenty-four are among the 3.3 million high school dropouts.
- Minorities comprise almost half the 1.3 million young discouraged workers expressing a desire for employment.
- Young Black men filled only one out of every 1,000 jobs created between 1970 and 1983.
- The labor-force participation rate for Black men declined from 83 per cent in 1960 to 61 per cent in 1983.

Perhaps the more fundamental reason that the youth unemployment crisis exists is because of the crisis of capital accumulation. In other words, increasing capital-intensive production has dislocated the labor-intensive workforce, tossing many Black youth aside and into the barrel of pauperism.

The Reagan administration promised an economic recovery and a balanced budget upon arriving in Washington. However, in the first three years of the administration, unemployment in the US reached the highest levels since the Great Depression. As a result, large numbers of wage-earners (previously considered middle class) joined the ranks of the working poor. In order to address this growing social contradiction, legislation was introduced by several congresspersons.

In September 1982, at the trough of the last recession, an emergency jobs bill was introduced by the Speaker of the House, Representative Thomas O'Neill, and co-sponsored in the Senate by Edward Kennedy. Passage of the bill would ensure the availability of $1 billion for the creation of 200,000 temporary jobs (up to six months in duration). The jobs would be located in the nation's infrastructural sector. The measure passed the house by a wide margin but was defeated by the more conservative Senate. Later, in October 1982, President Reagan signed into law the Jobs Training Partnership Act (JTPA) to replace the Comprehensive Employment Training Act (CETA) as the nation's primary federal employment and training legislation. JPTA was developed to assist the entry of youth and unskilled adults into the labor market. The differences between the JTPA and CETA are clear. First, JTPA was funded at just under $4 billion while CETA was previously funded at close to $9.5 billion. Second, JTPA was to be more reliant on the private sector for job placement.

After three years, JTPA continues to receive mixed reviews. Critics of the program express concern over its authority in allowing states to assume many functions previously performed by the US Department of Labor. On the local level, Private Industry Councils (PICs) perform many of JTPA's oversight functions, and receive little regulatory or targeting guidance. An independent sector assessment of JTPA programs conducted recently revealed the following:

- Eight per cent of the Service Delivery Areas surveyed are not meeting the legal requirements to spend 40 per cent of their funds on youth.
- Less than 6 per cent of the resources available for youth have been spent on remedial education activities.
- Despite the need to reach more youth, 48 per cent of the sites did not use the public schools as contractors for training and service for young people.

JTPA's programs were also plagued by restrictions on training stipends, effectively regulating those individuals with special needs, that is, childcare and transportation cost. Even if JTPA's programs were not plagued by restrictions, they could, at best, serve only 4 per cent of all the people eligible to participate.

African-American congressional representative Augustus Hawkins, Chairman of the House Education and Labor Sub-Committee, was among the first to recognize the ineffectiveness of JTPA strategies. Hawkins introduced in the 98th Congress the Youth Incentive Employment Act. The bill was designed to establish a program that would provide part-time school year and full-time summer employment to economically disadvantaged youth. The program would have produced jobs for unemployed youth between the ages of sixteen and nineteen who agreed to resume or maintain attendance in a high school or alternative educational or training program. The act would have authorized $2 billion for the creation of a million jobs.

The Youth Incentive Employment Act was also defeated. The debate over where funding would come from was a main reason. The introduction of a subminimum wage bill also insured its defeat. The "Youth Opportunity Wage" proposal was introduced in May 1984 to create a youth subminimum wage of $2.50, in contrast to the federal minimum wage of $3.35 (which has not been increased since 1981). The legislation, strongly backed by the Reagan administration, would have resulted in 16–19-year-olds receiving a youth differential during the summer months. The popular view that a low wage is better than no wage received wide coverage. Moreover, it was argued that for most young people, the $3.35 minimum wage greatly exceeds their production; hence, a second minimum wage would be logical and more equal to their level of productivity. The major objections to the legislation, in addition to its inability to address the real causes of youth unemployment, included the following factors:

- All available data suggest that a youth differential has little potential for reducing teenage unemployment.
- A youth subminimum wage would significantly reduce adult employment as most youth would be employed at the expense of the more than 7 million adult minimum wage workers.
- A youth differential represents a radical departure from the principle of equal pay for equal work regardless of race, sex, ethnic or national origin or age.

The subminimum wage proposal did not become law but it was able to gain broad support from very diverse political quarters, including the National Conference of Black Mayors. Currently, no basis exists for optimism relative to the passage of an enlightened federal employment policy unless a movement among the unemployed youth is developed.

The crisis of Black youth unemployment is exacerbated by government cutbacks in funding for job training programs. However, these programs also suffered from faulty conceptualization, planning and targeting. This was the conclusion of a study published by the Joint Center for Political and Economic Studies in Washington, DC.[12] The report states, furthermore,

> federal government support for formal education has declined. More emphasis has been put on state and local support . . . These changes would seem to be detrimental to black families, since blacks as a group may not receive the same level of support from state and local governments as they received from the federal government . . . In the area of training, comparable shifts have taken place.[13]

The authors of the 1987 Quality of Life Alternative Budget have asserted: "In a nation as affluent as the United States of America, the existence of poverty, illiteracy and a chronically high level of unemployment is an economic waste and human tragedy. It is a political disaster that suggests moral culpability on the part of those in office who inflict it, and the American citizens who permit it."[14] The economic waste and human tragedy among unemployed Black youth is usually termed marginalization. The social cost of youth marginalization, caused by deliberately imposed recession policies, can never be accurately calculated. However, several studies by noted researchers indicate that unemployment is closely linked to increases in crime, drug use and addiction, and illness (physical and mental). Furthermore, joblessness is strongly associated with depression, anxiety, aggression, insomnia, loss of self-esteem, marital problems, increased mental hospital admission and imprisonment. A number of studies indicate that the suicide rate for young men is correlated with cyclical unemployment, while increases in the homicide rate are related to high youth unemployment among prime age males.

Increased alienation is also a consequence of youth marginalization. This is reflected in high levels of high school dropouts, dramatic rises in Black suicide rates and the development of youth gangs. The alienation is heightened by the militarization of society. Black youths are being encouraged by a massive ideological campaign which exclaims that to "be all you can be" you simply have to join the Army, Air Force, Navy, and Marines. A byproduct of the alienation process is that a growing number of youths are beginning to blame themselves for being unemployed.

According to the report "The Value of Youth Work" released by the New York based group InterFace,

> The human costs of our failure to stem the rising tide of youth unemployment are immeasurable – particularly its contribution to family disintegration, personal anguish, social and economic deprivation, addiction and violence. In addition, there are the hard financial and economic costs of unemployment – costs borne by all taxpayers and the society as a whole. Public assistance benefits to unemployed youth cost the city $70 million a year. In terms of crime alone, the cost to the city's criminal justice system for 16–21 year olds amounts to $275 million a year.[15]

For Black youth, the consequences of chronic unemployment are devastating in all areas.[16] One of the more visible consequences is the growing number of young Black men and women (usually with small children) joining the ranks of America's homeless.[17] The growing trend in most urban and industrial centers (areas with high concentrations of African-Americans) is toward gentrification. When coupled with the increasing numbers of black youth who are pushed out on the streets as they leave institutions (such as foster care) and the declining supply of moderately priced housing, homelessness becomes a norm for a large sector of young people.

The National Urban League, commenting on the relationship between youth unemployment and homelessness, had this to say:

> For those of us who tried for so long to get this message across we wonder what it will take to arouse America from its lethargy. Back in 1976, the National Urban League called for a National Youth Employment Program, that included education, training and work components. Some critics called it visionary and complained of the price tag, but if it had been adopted many of the unemployed young men and women who now spend their days in idleness and hopelessness would be productive members of society. Those disadvantaged youngsters we were concerned with in 1976 are the young men and women of today. They grew up in poverty without the education and training they needed to make it in the world. Some of them have joined the recent American phenomenon of the homeless, eating in soup kitchens and sleeping in shelters or on outdoor grates warmed by whiffs of steam.[18]

Many conservatives state that they are baffled about why Blacks cannot make it in "pluralistic" America, given that other immigrant groups have made it. For them, the lack of values, the adoption of ghetto culture and unethical social behavior are the causes of the problem, not the nature of the capitalist system. The Black conservatives argue that the inculcation of middle-class values must take place among the youth. Dr Martin Luther King, Jr., had this to say about that approach:

> It is ironic that today so many educators and sociologists are seeking new methods to instill middle class values in Negro youth as the ideal in social development. It was precisely when young Negroes threw off their middle class values that they made an historic social contribution. They abandoned those values when they put careers and wealth in a secondary role . . . when they cheerfully became jailbirds and troublemakers. When they took off their Brooks Brothers attire and put on overalls to work in the isolated rural south.[19]

The new "blame the victim" critics of federally initiated social policy also assert that more self-help projects must be set up by Blacks, instead of depending on the government for handouts. Yet, no one who is familiar with the history of Black people in the United States could possibly suggest that they have not spent "many years, much energy and enormous resources engaged in self-help." Moreover, considering the level of the development of monopoly capitalism today, all the self-help projects that could be created in the Black community would not eliminate the complex array of problems confronting African-Americans. Additionally, to affirm the role and responsibility of the government to act in favor of enhancing the life opportunities of national minority groups does not in any way demean or negate individual initiative or self-improvement.

As we move toward the twenty-first century a real possibility exists that an entire generation of young African-Americans will have grown into adulthood without ever holding a job. Youth involvement and participation in the labor market certainly will depend on the growth of the US economy, and presently most projections forecast a slow rate of economic growth for the next few years. One wonders what such sluggishness will mean for the more than 25 per cent of young Black men who have never held a job.

According to the National Alliance of Businesses, jobs in the future will require higher skill levels than those of today and this will mean: "Employers will be demanding workers who are increasingly able to think and learn. Employers [will] also prefer to hire [workers who

have] either a post-secondary degree or three to four years experience."[20] To begin to address the unemployment situation in a more
futuristic manner, Congressman John Conyers has proposed reducing
the work week to thirty-two hours without a reduction in pay. In
introducing his legislation he stated:

> Today the nation faces a long-term unemployment problem that transcends
> cyclical changes in the economy. The use of fiscal and monetary policies to
> ease recessions cannot effectively solve the problem. The gap between
> economic recovery and employment recovery continues to widen with each
> subsequent recession. Unemployment rates at the peak of most economic
> cycles in the last 12 years have risen dramatically from 5 percent in the early
> 1970s, 9 percent in 1975 and close to 11 percent in the current cycle.
> Overshadowing the movement of particular business cycles is a long and
> developing structural change in the nature of production and work itself . . .
> Persistent high unemployment has degraded human skills and capabilities
> and damaged the fabric of society.[21]

The fabric of society most damaged has been Black youth. The
human misery and social degradation associated with the widespread
crisis of Black youth unemployment demands immediate attention and
action. The money required to purchase (at 1985 prices) twelve MX
missiles, ten B-1 bombers, eight F-15 fighters, and six M-1 tanks would
easily provide funding for a comprehensive youth employment and
community service program of national scope. Such a program could
link job training and education by making the former a third semester
and component part of the latter. Hence, in the short run we must
support legislation such as that introduced by Representatives Hawkins and Conyers, as well as develop creative alternatives on the local
level. However, we must realize that such programs will not solve the
problem of youth unemployment. America is in need of profound
structural transformation that will eliminate unemployment totally.

Exactly what does the future hold for African-American youth? All
important indicators point to the continued existence of limited job
opportunities, poor educational preparation and increased national
oppression. Commenting on this bleak picture, the National Alliance
of Businesses has warned that: "If we fail to solve these problems
during this window of opportunity we can expect to enter the next
century with social and economic problems that are worse than those
of today. Not only are higher crime and welfare dependency rates likely
but radical or violent political or social action could result."[22]

Conclusion

The crisis of Black youth unemployment does not exist in isolation from other profound changes taking place in the society. The impact of the present socio-economic conditions on Black youth is physically and psychologically devastating. The crisis of Black youth unemployment, when correctly characterized, amounts to "economic genocide."

Today's youth marginalization is the result of policies deliberately imposed by the Reagan and Bush administrations to insure the existence of a profitable climate for multinational corporations. This crisis and the impact it is having on all youth, African-American youth in particular, is exacerbated by the militarization of the US economy. The major expression of this phenomenon is defense spending; here lie the roots of the stepped-up arms race and the social basis for the promotion of an anti-communist foreign policy.

The author challenges the apologists of the capitalist system and conservative critics of an "enlightened social policy" on the issue of their racist, cultural determinist views which suggest that behavior and values are the cause of the present crisis confronting African-American youth. Behavior and values do not exist apart from the environment, nor does the environment exist apart from the broader society. There is a definite relationship between one's social situation and one's social behavior, but that relationship is dictated by forces much greater than young people who smoke marijuana or engage in pre-marital sex.

Notes

1. Keith Jennings, "Fact Sheet on Youth Unemployment Job Training" (Washington, DC: National Student Education Fund, September 1984).

2. "A Nation Apart," *U.S. News and World Report* (March 17, 1986), p. 18.

3. *The State of Black America* (New York: National Urban League, 1986), p. 214.

4. *The Nature of Youth Unemployment: An Analysis for Policymakers* (Paris: Organization for Economic Corporation and Development Publications, 1984), pp. 1–5.

5. Barry Bluestone, "Deindustrialization and Unemployment in America," *Review of Black Political Economy* (Fall 1983), pp. 27–42.

6. Ibid., pp. 30–31.

7. "Debunking the Myth," Full Employment Action Council, July 14, 1984.

8. *The Quality of Life Alternative Budget: Fiscal 1987* (Washington, DC: Congressional Black Caucus), pp. 13–14.

9. Bluestone, "Deindustrialization," p. 30.

10. Manning Marable, "The Crisis of the Black Working Class, An Economic and Historical Analysis," *Science and Society* (Summer 1982), p. 156.

11. Ibid., p. 57.

12. See Marguerite C. Simms, *Black Economic Progress: An Agenda for the 1990s* (Washington, DC: Joint Center for Political and Economic Studies, 1988), pp. 31–7 and p. 8.

13. Ibid., p. 9.

14. *The Quality of Life Alternative Budget: Fiscal Year 1987*, p. 57.

15. *The Value of Youth Work* (New York: InterFace, 1984), p. 3.

16. Ibid., p. 58.

17. Ibid., p. 55.

18. *The State of Black America*, p. iii.

19. Martin Luther King, Jr., Speech to Staff, Southern Christian Leadership Conference (November 1967).

20. *Youth 2000* (Washington, DC: National Alliance of Business, 1986), p. 5.

21. *Congressional Record* (February 23, 1983), p. E594–5.

22. *Youth 2000*, p. 7.

11

The Role of Land and African-Centered Values in Black Economic Development

Lloyd Hogan

African-Americans have come a long way. From primordial beginnings on the African soil some three million years ago, they evolved as isolated members of human families with few interconnections outside of their immediate households. At some critical juncture in their evolution they yielded up the exclusive dominion of family life to the supremacy of the clan. Hand in hand with this development came the effective transformation of African family labor into clan social labor. Members of the society now labored in common to satisfy their individual and social needs. No outside human agents dictated the terms on which they could exercise their labors in the production of their material survival needs; nor did any such agent dictate their quantitative share in the material results of their labor. Only the natural proclivities of the larger earth environment presented challenges to be overcome as they went about their daily chores. A classless society of Black men, women, and children thereby subsisted in dynamic harmony with the African earth.

Throughout the continent such a revolution was repeated thousands of times. A corresponding number of different peoples emerged, each stamped with its own cultural identity, distinct languages, a peculiar mode of socialization of their young, a unique generational binding mythology, and a special way of living. The harmonious existence in world history that these African communal societies enjoyed, however, ultimately was invaded by outside human agents. Some of these agents were domestic to the African continent; but the most momentous assault came from a band of alien invaders from across the seas to inflict the most vicious disruption of the communal life. In conspiracy with some native African merchant marauders and feudal satraps the aliens enslaved the communalists, shipped them across the ocean as living cargo in the holds of their ships, and made them work the plantations of the Americas for the private benefits of other alien masters.

This transformation of the African communalists into African-American slaves required several conditions for its successful completion. These conditions are still relevant for understanding the political economy of Black communities in America today. First, the African communalists were appropriated as the private property of European entrepreneurs. Second, the marauders seized private ownership and control of the slaves' *internal labor process*. And thirdly, they determined the *external labor process* of the African.[1] Controlling the internal and external labor processes was not sufficient for complete control and exploitation of the Africans by the European and native white exploiters. In order to insure the unified and uninterrupted exertion of all phases of slave labor, the owner completely dictated to the slave all the conditions under which labor would take place. These conditions effectively set the legitimate rate of exploitation of the slaves at fully 100 per cent of the fruits of their labors.

In time, the African-American slaves were freed. They now entered upon a new existence as landless peasant sharecroppers. The croppers achieved partial control of their internal labor process. However, the uninterrupted and unified exertion of both phases of the croppers' labor required the "voluntary" acquiescence of the croppers in an agreement which bound them for life to landless status upon the land. Such agreements established the legal basis for the white landlords to expropriate the major portion of the fruits of the croppers' labor.[2] Thus, the croppers subsisted in abject poverty in spite of the rigors of their labor.

In recent decades the African-American sharecroppers were liberated from the shackles of the sharecropping system and were transformed into wage laborers. Certain economic and political conditions defined this new social arrangement. Black wage laborers won the right to control their internal labor.[3] The uninterrupted and unified exertion of both phases of Black wage labor required the "voluntary" submission of both white capitalists and the African-American wage laborers to market rules of distribution. These rules fixed the legitimate terms under which the African-American wage laborers might have the opportunity to exert *external labor*. The rules also fixed the quantity of the material fruits of external labor which would be returned to the laborers for their personal use in internal labor.

These dramatic historic transformations of the African-American population point to progressive trends in the conditions of these people. They were enslaved in the beginning; but they won their freedom. Personal freedom persisted throughout the next two succeeding social revolutions. In the last transformation, in addition to their personal freedom, they also won some control over their *internal labor process*. But they still have no power to make decisions about the quantity, extent and consequential products of *internal labor*. As a matter of fact, their so-called voluntary market decisions place them in a situation where the very nature and extent of their internal labor (which they own and control) must respond in lock-step fashion to the ravages inflicted upon them in the external labor process (which is still owned by white capitalists).

The future course is clear. Members of the African-American wage laboring population must, at all costs, maintain possession of their personal freedom. This is the *sine qua non* of their future existence. And it is not clear that this is a given. There is a growing number of Black youth subsisting in prisons. There are other assaults against Black civil rights, parading under the guise of cleansing the Black community of drugs and crime. African-Americans cannot take their personal freedom for granted in today's America. Second, they must maintain ownership, and strive for complete control, of their *internal labor process*. The quantity, extent and result of this phase of their labor must be grounded in the principle of the creation of an African-American laboring population which is molded in the true spirit of humanity. Third, they must move forward politically to challenge their historic condition of powerlessness by seizing ownership and control of their *external labor process*. No longer should external class interests dictate the extent, nature and result of the phase of labor which produces the material means of their survival.

These conditions are necessary for liberation from the exploitative machinations of the existing capitalist reproductive relations that confine the Black community to subservient economic, social and cultural status. African-Americans must resist and dismantle the market institutions and arrangements which now fix the terms of their exploitation. Market principles are the epitome of capitalist private property relations. These principles must give way to assignment of tasks in the external labor process based on the personal talents which inhere in each African-American individual.[4] At the same time, each individual must receive a quantity and kind of material goods based on that individual's needs. The new principle of distribution, however, has to be tempered by collective social goals that are democratically determined.

In short, the future program for African-Americans requires the demise of the capitalist mode of exploitation of their labors. It also entails the construction of a new social order based on personal freedom, equal opportunity, the inalienable right to participate in the creation of the material means of survival, and the effective right to acquire quantities and types of material means of survival based purely on individual need.

At the present time African-Americans constitute less than 12 per cent of the population in the United States. They operate in an environment in which the white members of the general wage working class are rather backward in terms of conscious understanding of common interests which indelibly bind them to their African-American wage-laboring brothers and sisters.[5] African-Americans also subsist under rules promulgated and enforced by a not too friendly (if not totally repressive) political state. Furthermore, a good number of African-Americans still hold out the hopes of surviving with dignity within the bowels of the present national capitalist order. They believe that in time they will be able to achieve capitalist or at least near-capitalist status; or they hope they will be able to penetrate the upper levels of the wage distribution. More schooling, affirmative action inroads into the upper reaches of the hierarchy of control within the division of labor, more intensive involvement in capitalist party political affairs, stepping up the pace and establishment of Black-owned business enterprise – these and other policies and strategies are relied on to bring about the millennium within the existing capitalist social relations.

Today African-Americans are still exploited to a greater degree than their non-Black counterparts. Average wage payments, and consequently average acquisition of the material means of survival, place African-Americans at about 70 per cent of the living standard of white workers. The brutal result of this is that African-Americans experience a greater rate of decay of their potential population; that is to say, they die off much more rapidly. These and other factors may present obstacles to the African-American quest for freedom. Yet the developing realities of life in the United States may help to paint a clearer picture of the future.

It must be understood that the two great revolutions – slavery to sharecropping, sharecropping to wage laboring – were won by African-Americans themselves. Yet there is still a universality of thought, even among African-Americans, that somehow African-Americans have been passive receptacles into which historical change has flowed. This myth must be challenged; the notion of a passive African-American community goes hand in hand with social, cultural, and economic exploitation.

This notion dies hard. Many African-Americans believe that it was Northern capitalist armed might which gave the decisive death blow to slavery. The stimulus for this military campaign, it is believed, originated partly out of the moral indignation of leading abolitionists and partly out of the economic interests of the Northern capitalists. An integral part of this thinking is that revolutions which come from the downtrodden are struck by heroic deeds of brave individuals. Black slave revolts did occur, they say; but they were soon put down. The heroes were there, but alas they did not succeed. In the case of the destruction of the feudal sharecropping relations absolutely nothing is said about the decisive role of the Black migrant from the land. That revolutionary worker on the road toward social transformation was believed to be the source of Black urban problems, rather than conceived of as the carrier of historic metamorphoses in social relations.

While there is a modicum of truth in current thought it is nevertheless a most incomplete view of the facts. It was a result of African-American efforts throughout their history that brought on revolutionary changes. The heroes of the piece are the nameless millions of men, women, and children – all African-American – whose births, and lives, and deaths now enrich the American soil. If there is one theme which dominates our view of history it is precisely that the liberating force of all exploited classes is the exertion of human labor. Labor is the critical activity which makes a people's survival possible. It creates both the material means of their survival as well as the people themselves. The fact that it has existed under exploitative pressures, generally manifested brutally in the characteristic distribution mechanisms, is precisely the dynamic which brings about change in society.

The greater the degree of exploitation, the greater must be the exertion of human labor if the population is to survive. But the greater the exertion of human labor, the greater is the opportunity for increased levels of exploitation. The one feeds upon the other. But continually the explosive character of the increasing intensity of human labor must reach a magnitude that defies the existing distributional mechanism to contain it. This is indeed the fundamental nature of the internal contradiction which inheres in any given social order. The brutality of slave labor and its extremely large toll in Black lives must have been matched by an extraordinary effort of Black slaves to survive. They not only survived, but by the end of the Civil War they were reproducing themselves at an increasing rate. A similar survival result followed the demise of the sharecropping system. In short, "survivability" of the African-American people, under the most excruciating social and economic circumstances, has been one of their most indomitable traits.

The problem for African-Americans has been that on each occasion, in the cases of the two social revolutions which they won through their own efforts, an opportunistic external ruling class stood at the ready to ensnare them into a new exploitative labor system. So was it in the case of the Southern landlords after the freeing of the slaves. So too was it in the case of the capitalists at the liberation of the sharecropper.

At the consummation of both social revolutions no African-American ruling class was spawned by the political and economic upheavals. African-Americans continued as a homogeneous American working class, but with their African identity remaining intact. The essential meaning of this is that in no important sense can we separate out of African origin the only sensible interpretation of what people mean by race and class status of African-Americans. African-Americans have been, throughout their American experience, of African origin and simultaneously a working class – African-American slaves, African-American sharecroppers, African-American wage laborers. This alone would separate the experiences of Blacks from immigrant groups of European origin. And this places the African-American community in *the* historical vanguard position for revolutionary social change in America, and the world.

Despite the unique experiences of African-Americans, today they cannot be viewed as isolated from other exploited sectors. The two great social revolutions were won at times when the non-Black working class was of a different historical mold than their Black counterparts. African-American slaves existed in the same real time interval alongside non-Black landless peasants; African-American sharecroppers shared the same real time interval with non-Black sharecroppers, non-Black independent peasants, non-Black wage workers. There is no way now, however, to isolate the class of African-American wage laborers from the general class of wage laborers. The social division of labor manifested in cooperation between African-American and non-Black wage laborers across the nation, and the national process of capital accumulation itself, have erased any important objective distinguishing characteristics of the two segments of the working class.

Finally, African-Americans have not yet exercised what modicum of personal freedom they possess to forge more formal relationships with the many African nations of their origin. They are increasing their individual contacts with specific African nations and African nationals.

They have tried to bring some of their concerns to the Organization of African Unity and to organs of the United Nations. Thus, African-Americans are becoming more conscious of the international impact of their struggle for freedom.

A new social revolution is now in progress. In the near future it is possible to project Black survival rates approaching that of the nation as a whole. It should be obvious that the start of the African-American wage labor system represented a significant decline in the rate of exploitation, and this should translate directly into increased survival. Already, the blackening of the large cities across the nation previews this momentous event. This revolution is proceeding apace in step with the rate of capital accumulation upon the backs of the African-American population. Legally stolen African-American labor, transformed into non-Black material wealth, spells the physical death of the African-American population. But that same process signals the extent of the corresponding intensification of African-American internal labor to overcome the ravages of death. A significant component of that internal labor is indeed the development of a consciousness within the Black community to eradicate the social source of its exploitation.

Inherent in the internal labor of the African-American population is the source for creation of a surplus African-American population over and beyond the exploitative needs of capital. This is reflected in the growing absolute magnitude of unemployed African-Americans who represent the "freeing up" of African-Americans from the binding forces of the capitalist market mechanism. Unemployment among members of the African-American population could be part of a process that portends growing liberation of these people from direct capitalist exploitative mechanisms. Rather than bemoan this empirical reality, it therefore becomes extremely urgent that an African-American "safety net" be installed by the people themselves to capture these unemployed workers so that they can be used in the progressive political and cultural interests of African-Americans. No longer should these people have the coming of a new social revolution slowed by either the external class interests, or by their uncommitted Black leaders. The critical issue now before Black activists and leadership is how to organize those sectors in the Black community who have been discarded by American capitalism, and how to approach this sector not as pathology or problems of economic dislocation, but as important resources in the struggle to finally gain control of Black internal and external labor processes. The principles governing the nature of the net were laid out above.

The net must preserve Black personal freedom. Many know this under the rubric of "civil rights." Many know this under the rubric of a "right" to a decent standard of living. The net must give to African-American households complete control of their internal labor process. The net must give to African-American households complete control over their external labor process. This latter characteristic of the net is the most decisive change of status which the social revolution requires. In practical terms, this condition requires that African-American households devise their own system for the creation of their material means of survival. First and foremost, external labor must serve the production of the elementary material means of survival – their continuing food requirements. At the present time this works out to about twenty million metric tonnes annually and will increase at an annual amount of about two hundred thousand metric tonnes. The composition in terms of different types of food and the corresponding nutritive substances is implicit in this kind of discussion.

Food can be produced only by the exertion of external labor. Common ownership of land thus becomes indispensable. Land ownership is fairly well understood throughout the African-American community. However, with the exception of the Republic of New Africa, most African-Americans are ambiguously committed to the concept. To many of them, landed existence conjures up the old sharecropping days and the associated backwardness of the rural life. These ideas must be overcome by making the land question an important consciousness raising activity of the highest priority. Acquisition of common ownership of the three million acres now privately owned by African-Americans and the common acquisition of more land in the continental United States are essential parts of this program.

Food production for meeting the continuing requirements of the African-American population is absolutely essential. This means, of course, that the control of land, both urban and rural, is, *ipso facto*, absolutely essential. Beyond this, organizing to produce the other material requirements for survival must hinge on what is done about the food question. Implementation of the food program in the right way sets the necessary basis for the production of the other material means of survival. In any case, the organization and implementation of the food program must begin with the material means of production – the land – collectively owned. The second requisite is to marshal the subjective element of consciously directed labor out of the large number of African-Americans who form an ever increasing part of the reserve army of the unemployed in the United States.

Let's be clear about whom we speak. For purposes of political mobilization and developing incipient strategies of Black economic liberation from capitalism the unemployed African-Americans with whom we are immediately concerned cannot be associated with the problems of this or that specific firm or industry business cycle. African-Americans not sharing the nation's wealth and well-being are victims of the national process of capital accumulation. They are the living human manifestations of the internal contradictions of the capitalist political economy. It is indeed these African Americans who join the reserve army of the unemployed at the rate of half a million annually without ever gaining any employment status whatsoever. How to organize these youth for productive existence in the new social order presents the great and impending challenge to Black activists and leadership.

Many reform approaches must be pursued simultaneously to ease the burdens of the people while pursuing the major strategy. These should be guided by the principle of denying to the capitalist exploiters, at opportune moments, the right to steal Black labor. In order to safeguard the current status of the people we must turn to the organization of politically oriented labor associations and progressive caucuses within unions, cementing the bonds of unity among welfare mothers at the local and national level, and seeking more self-determination and community control in the running of schools and other municipal institutions; in fact, the strengthening of political and social organizations that prioritize the well-being of people must be the major strategy for the improvement of the quality of life in Black communities.

Finally, African-Americans must use their international kinship ties. Recall that African-Americans constitute one of the largest African nations in the world, even though they have no African geographical base. The African connection has to be revived and strengthened. A process of diplomatic negotiations with the nations of the African continent must be initiated under which each nation reserves a block of territory for the unencumbered settlement of African-Americans. A general OAU resolution, coupled with specific enabling pacts with each African nation, based on its own peculiar circumstances, should be pursued. This could well provide a threat to the established order that if it doesn't shape up, the African-Americans may still exercise the option to secede.

Notes

1. Detailed explanations of the two labor processes mentioned are to be found in Lloyd Hogan, *Principles of Black Political Economy* (Boston: Routledge and Kegan Paul, 1984).

2. The standard agreement called for a 50–50 sharing of the product of the cropper's labor. The empirical reality saw the average cropper's share reduced to the absolute minimum food requirements for survival. The lion's share went to the landlord. While a few croppers did fairly well, the majority experienced debt peonage for the rest of their lives.

3. This is the meaning of the "legal" acquisition of civil rights in the 1960s.

4. Refer to the article by Jeremiah Cotton in Chapter 1 of this volume. Cotton makes a convincing case for the abject failure of the market mechanism to provide adequate jobs and pay opportunities for African-Americans.

5. The economic and political advantages enjoyed by white workers are well documented throughout the various chapters of this volume. The fear of losing their jobs and other advantages can explain much of the backwardness of this segment of the working class.

Conclusion

Richard Hatcher

The major issue demanding the attention of African-Americans today is whether we are effectively using our political power to create an environment and climate which will permit an expansion of an economic base for community development – not an economic base to produce a few millionaires, or guarantee a certain number of Black families middle-class status, but an economic base that means social development for the entire community.

This question has been confronted collectively by the essays in this volume. Critical questions, and important criticisms of the state of public policy and race, and economic development, have been raised by the contributors. I will touch upon only a few of the issues raised here, and also utilize the framework that is expressed by the contributors to suggest yet another idea for Black economic development in the current period.

Over the last twenty years African-American representation has risen from "no mayors" of major American cities to more than three hundred. The number of Black elected officials has grown from two to three hundred elected officials in 1972 to more than 6,000 by 1989. At the state and local levels African-Americans have been increasing their numbers and their influence in state legislatures throughout America. In a few states like California and Illinois, individual African-American legislators have achieved exalted positions of leadership and power. Colorado and California produced the first Black lieutenant governors since Reconstruction and several other states like Michigan and Connecticut saw the election of Blacks to statewide offices such as treasurer and auditor. Finally, the ultimate prize at the state level has been seized. Doug Wilder, a Black man, has been elected governor of the state of Virginia – a remarkable accomplishment in a state with such a long history of racial oppression.

At the same time that the above electoral advances are being realized, however, the economic status of African-Americans has worsened. Somehow, the substantial political progress of Blacks must be translated into meaningful economic progress. The Black community has not yet been able to do this, primarily because it has been fettered by liberal and conservative approaches to issues dealing with economic development.

Historically, American ethnic groups have established their political power for the specific purpose of achieving economic power. They understood, from the outset, that politics is not an end in, and of, itself; rather, it is a means to an end. The Irish in Chicago and Boston, the Italians in Newark and the Germans in Milwaukee all understood this basic principle. Apparently, African-Americans are still learning this important lesson in a socially and economically bitter way. Many of us do not yet seem to make the connection between political empowerment and economic empowerment. Black businesspersons and Black politicians rarely talk to each other – this is meant both figuratively and substantively. One is focused on getting elected or re-elected and the other is trying to make a profit. It's as if these two things were polar opposites, when in fact they represent areas of mutual interest and involvement.

As was ultimately reflected by the civil rights movement in the sixties, and the Black Power movement in the seventies, we are now in a period of needing economic rights; this means that we must find a way to leverage our hard-earned political muscle and clout into economic benefits and advances for African-American people. We should not apologize or be philosophically defensive about this necessity. As stated earlier every other ethnic group in America has not hesitated to use political power to help their own, economically speaking. A casual reading of American history confirms this claim. We must reject the claim of some neo-conservatives – and liberals – that Blacks do not need political power, or that this kind of power is unrelated to economic power. This claim is simply ahistorical in America. We must also reject the claim of some liberals that while political power is important, it should be lodged in the hands of those who will push "national" programs, and who will not scare away white citizens with talk of Black political influence. We cannot afford to let other interests represent our interests; this, too, is an axiom of American politics that other racial and ethnic groups have adhered to religiously.

There are certain guideposts that African-Americans should consider in order to utilize political strength to increase economic advancement and improve social welfare in the 1990s. These guideposts are reflected in the essays in this volume. First, we must seek to expand the arena or boundaries of public policy in order to consider alternative means to achieve what traditional liberal or conservative means have failed to do. African-Americans cannot confine themselves to debating only liberal and conservative approaches to economic development at the local level.

Perhaps the possibility of an African-American "Institute of Politics" should be considered in order to insure the representation of alternative perspectives regarding matters of public policy and community economic development. The AAIOP could function as both a theoretical and a pragmatic training institution for young African-Americans who aspire to public service and elective offices throughout the country and at all levels of government. Very practical courses on how to organize a political campaign and/or a voter registration drive would be coupled with serious analytical and philosophical discussions regarding African-American public policy. The AAIOP could also recruit political practitioners from different levels of government to discuss their experiences and ideas. Such an institute would eventually exercise significant influence on public policy in Black America. One has only to consider the tremendous influence wielded by Harvard University's Institute of Politics, to understand the great potential such an institution represents for the African-American community. Today every new African-American mayor of a large city and every new African-American member of Congress along with their white counterparts is routinely brought to Harvard for a week of political and economic "indoctrination." The Black intellectual and activist community should consider something similar to this for Black mayors and elected officials. We must make our political representatives understand the value and benefit of creative thinking and approaches; we could have a major impact on public policy in urban America for everyone if forums were available to entertain the experiences and insights of Black activists and political officials.

Another area that we must address if we are to reach political and economic parity with our fellow white citizens by the year 2000 has to do with national and state legislatures. African-Americans are at least thirty million and more strong in the United States and yet we may be the only group which does not have a formal lobby in Washington, DC, protecting our economic and social interests on *a-day-to-day* basis. We are fortunate that civil rights organizations like the NAACP and Urban League allocate some of their limited resources to this task. What would we as a people have done without Clarence Mitchell, Althea Simmons, Maudine Cooper and others, who fought and are fighting our battles on Capitol Hill? Today, however, when our needs and interests have moved beyond civil rights issues as such, we need a fully constituted African-American lobby to address our concerns on Capitol Hill and in state legislatures around the country.

Finally, the conversion of African-American political power into meaningful economic development calls for the development of a "Black Common Market." The idea for this kind of effort is patterned after some of the principles, practices and institutions of the European Economic Community (EEC), which was founded in the aftermath of World War II. Its central tenet is "for the common good" of all its member nations. The four major features of Black economic community in the United States would be:

1. *Collective purchasing* by member cities, agencies and private member entities.
2. *Division of labor* or specialization by its member cities.
3. *An African-American development loan fund*, to finance and foster minority ownership, skill development and training, education and political development and advocacy.
4. *Trade with foreign countries*, particularly with those in Africa and the Caribbean.

Regarding this last point, collective trade with these countries could be established on a mutually beneficial basis, further expanding the markets of companies providing goods and services in Black common market member cities. In addition, each member city could establish free-trade zones, where foreign nations needing locations near American companies doing business with them could be sited. The Black common market would organize trade missions to visit other countries and develop both import and export businesses.

The economic rise of Europe from the destruction of World War II is as much the result of European organization and cooperation as American post-war aid. American aid was a boon to European nations, but more importantly they worked together to rebuild economic prosperity. There is a parallel here for African-Americans: they must complement aid (federal programs, and so on) with self-won economic gains (capital accumulation, investments, and so on) through co-operation. The African-American community must move beyond governmental paternalism and develop the strategy and resources for Blacks to seize control of the benefits of government. We should not reject assistance from government, and instead advocate for more of it as does every organized interest in this nation. But we should also insist that these benefits are organized and distributed in ways that we feel will benefit our communities economically, socially and politically.

The components of the Black common market would include co-operative purchasing, division of labor and specialization, development of a loan fund based on contributions from African-American communities, and trade relations with foreign countries. African-American political leaders and entrepreneurs oriented towards the revitalization of African-American communities would begin to work together in order to establish the Black common market. The need for a Black common market and new approach for Black economic development is clear. Over the last twenty years, African-Americans have slowly but surely increased their influence within America's local governments, particularly in cities. This idea, if institutionalized, will allow African-Americans to expand their influence on local economics, control their own destiny and help create parity with other racial and ethnic groups in the United States.

Various essays in this collection suggest other ideas and strategies that could improve the economic conditions of Blacks in America. All the essays grope for answers that are based on the political mobilization of the Black community, and on strategies that acknowledge cultural strengths in this community. All those interested in developing or implementing public policy geared towards ameliorating depressed socio-economic conditions should examine these essays for approaches and values that are yet to be reflected in public policy, but could very well help generate the kinds of policies and strategies that will enhance the economic vibrancy and viability of Black America.

Contributors

Sheila Ards is an Assistant Professor at the Hubert Humphrey Institute, University of Minnesota. She teaches courses in social policy analysis; her research interests include child abuse, welfare, and housing policies.

Jeremiah Cotton is an Associate Professor of Economics at the University of Massachusetts/Boston. His articles have appeared in *The Review of Economics and Statistics*, *The American Journal of Economics and Sociology*, *Review of Black Political Economy*, and *Social Science Quarterly*.

William Fletcher is a former labor organizer for District 65-United Auto Workers. He is associate editor of *Forward Motion* magazine. He is the co-author of *The Indispensable Ally: Black Workers and the Formation of the Congress of Industrial Organizations, 1934–1941*.

Richard Hatcher was the first Black mayor of Gary, Indiana, serving between 1967 and 1983. He was also one of the convenors and organizers of the National Black Political Convention in 1972 as well as an advisor to the Jesse Jackson presidential campaigns in 1984 and 1988.

Charles P. Henry is Associate Professor of Afro-American Studies at the University of California/Berkeley. He is the author of two recent books: *Culture and African American Politics* and *The Search for Common Ground: Jesse Jackson's Campaigns for President*.

Lloyd Hogan is currently Visiting Professor of Economics at Elizabeth City State University. He was the Editor of *Review of Black Political Economy* for several years covering volumes 4 to 11. He is author of *Principles of Black Political Economy*.

James Jennings is Professor of Political Science, and Director of the

William Monroe Trotter Institute at the University of Massachusetts/ Boston. His publications include *The Politics of Black Empowerment*, *Puerto Rican Politics in Urban America* and *From Access to Power*.

Keith Jennings is an activist who has spoken in many countries around the world on issues of race, peace, and human rights. He is currently the Deputy Director of the Southern region of the USA of Amnesty International.

Mack Jones is Professor of Political Science at Prairie View A&M University. His area of specialty is race and Southern politics. He is the author of numerous books and of articles appearing in *Political Science Quarterly*, *Daedalus*, *The Annals*, *The Review of Black Political Economy*, and others.

Julianne Malveaux is an economist and syndicated columnist. Her publications include *Black Working Women: Debunking the Myths*, chapters in *Labor Economics: Modern Views, The Year Left 2*, and other books, as well as articles in numerous professional journals.

Eugene 'Gus' Newport is the former Executive Director of the Dudley Street Neighborhood Initiative, a community-based housing and community development agency in Boston, Massachusetts. Mr Newport is also the former mayor of Berkeley, California, serving between the years 1978 and 1986. He is known internationally for his work on behalf of peace and economic development.

Jacqueline Pope is Associate Professor of Political Science at Stocton State College. She is the author of *Biting the Hand that Feeds Them*, as well as numerous articles and essays focusing on the experiences of women on public assistance. She worked closely with the National Welfare Rights Organization.

Walter Stafford is Associate Professor of Planning and Public Administration at New York University. His research and writing focuses on racial experiences in the labor market. He is the author of numerous publications and is currently completing a study on the politicization of underclass sectors in New York City.

Index

THE HAYMARKET SERIES

Already Published

Forthcoming

THE INVENTION OF THE WHITE RACE
Theodore Allen

THE ARCHITECTURE OF COMPANY TOWNS
Margaret Cameron

SHADES OF NOIR
Edited by Mike Davis and Joan Copjec

THE MERCURY THEATER: Orson Welles and the Popular Front
Michael Denning

THE POLITICS OF SOLIDARITY: Central America and the US Left
Van Gosse

BLACK RADICAL TRADITIONS
Cynthia Hamilton

BLACK AMERICAN POLITICS: From the Washington Marches to Jesse
Jackson (Second Edition)
Manning Marable

WHITE GUYS
Fred Pfeil

AMERICAN DOCUMENTARY FILM
Paula Rabinowitz

THE GROUNDING OF INTELLECTUALS
Bruce Robbins

FEMINISM IN THE AMERICAS
The Year Left 5